CW00403543

Speaking With an American Accent:
A Guide to General American English Pronunciation
Kari Lim, M.S., CCC-SLP

Copyright © 2022 Independently published
All rights reserved. This book or any portion thereof
may not be reproduced or used in any manner whatsoever
without the express written permission of the author
except for the use of brief quotations in a book review.

Printed in the United States of America

First Printing, 2022

ISBN 9798410300698

www.GlobalSpeechTherapy.com

Table of Contents

Section

1

Introduction

Copyright © 2022

A Note from the Author

The purpose of the book is to give professionals and clients a place to get started with accent acquisition/modification so that they have an idea of topics addressed, explanations and examples of those topics in General American English (GenAm), and practice stimuli. You are prompted to add in your own materials or preferred client stimuli. Professionals and clients can apply these principles and formats discussed in this book to learning any accent or dialect. I wish you all the best in your journey in accent modification!

About the Author

Kari Lim has been a practicing Speech-Language Pathologist since 2005. She has a range of clinical experience and has worked in various settings, including home health, public schools, and hospitals.

Kari has a strong interest in international collaboration and has worked in several capacities with organizations abroad. She has mentored, taught, and supervised students and practitioners in Mexico, Zambia, Guyana, Ghana, and Cambodia.

Since 2011, Kari has been a clinical supervisor at The George Washington University in the Department of Speech, Language, and Hearing Sciences, where she created the study abroad program for the department. She has led programs in Mexico, Nepal, and South Korea.

Her areas of expertise are accent modification, professional speaking, autism, language development, articulation, and international collaboration. Kari has served in many roles in professional organizations, including the D.C. Speech-Language-Hearing Association (DCSHA) and the Council of State Association Presidents (CSAP). She is a recipient of the 2016 Ten Outstanding Young Americans award.

Dedication

A huge thank you to family, friends, and colleagues who gave me support, encouragement, and guidance along the way as I strive to meet my goals and live by the words of Eleanor Roosevelt "You must do the things you think you cannot do." For our baby Kaiya Grace, we will hold you in our hearts until we can hold you in Heaven.

The author took all steps to contact copyright holders regarding material, request permission, and cite sources referenced. If any source was inadvertently overlooked, please reach out to the author and corrections will be made at the first opportunity.

Terms of Use

Thank you for your purchase! By purchasing this resource, you agree that the contents are the property of Kari Lim and licensed to you only for professional/personal use as a single user. Kari Lim retains the copyright and reserves all rights to this product.

You May:
- Use content in this book for your students/clients or your personal use.
- Reference this product in blog posts, seminars, professional development workshops, and other venues ONLY if credit is given to me as the author with a link back to my Amazon store.

You May Not:
- Claim this work as your own
- Sell the files or combine them into another unit for sale/free.
- Post this document for sale/free elsewhere on the internet.
- Make or send copies to share with others.
- All of this is strictly forbidden and violates the Terms of Use/law.

Thank you for abiding by universally accepted codes of professional ethics while using this product.

For questions, feedback, or inquiries about accent coaching or public speaking, please email me at Kari@GlobalSpeechTherapy.Com.

Thank you,
Kari Lim, M.S., CCC-SLP

There is a companion website that contains downloadable Word documents of the assessment materials and practice stimuli for you and your own clients.

**IN BACK OF BOOK
SEE SUMMARY SECTION FOR DETAILS**

Section

2

Accents and Dialects

<u>Accents vs. Dialects</u>

Everyone has an accent! There is no standard language or accent spoken across the world. Even within each country, there are many variations of a spoken language. These variations are commonly referred to as a dialect, and it's typically specific to a particular region or group of people. As a result, the thing on wheels at the grocery store is referred to as 'buggy' in the southern part of the United States (U.S.) and 'cart' in the northern part. In the U.S., there are approximately 24 regional dialects, which have been influenced over the years by geographical boundaries, socioeconomic backgrounds, generational changes, ethnicity and race, and other individual factors. A great visual representation of U.S. regional dialects is *The Dialect Map of U.S. English* from Robert Delaney in Figure 2-1. This map shows that there are more dialectal variations on the East Coast vs. West Coast of the U.S.

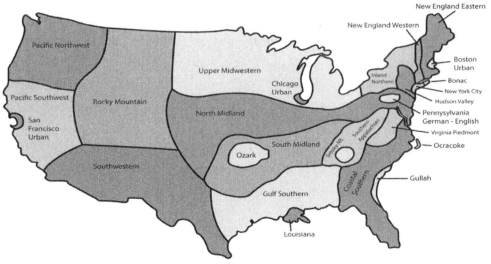

Figure 2-1. Delaney, R. (2013).

Regional dialect is just one category of dialects. There are also ethnic dialects, which are dialects spoken by members of a particular ethnic group. The two most known ethnic dialects in the U.S. are African American Vernacular English (AAVE) and Chicano English (or Hispanic Vernacular). Most speakers of these dialects are monolingual and live in urban areas around the U.S.

Humans are wired to learn any language or accent at birth. We learn a language, and therefore an accent, through listening, play, and practice. Although many people speak three or more languages, for the ease of simplicity, in this book, a language other than the native language (L1) is referred to as a 2nd language (L2). Factors that influence an accent are:
- The age at which the L2 was mastered
- If the language teachers had a native accent
- How closely related L1 and L2 are in terms of speech sounds and grammar
- Frequency of practice and exposure to L2
- How well the speaker has mastered the L2

Although accent and dialect are often used interchangeably, the true definition of accent is the unique way speech is pronounced by a group of people speaking the same language (American Speech-Language-Hearing Association, n.d.). A dialect is not only how sounds are pronounced, but also the vocabulary and grammar that are used.

A nonnative accent occurs when a person speaks their 2nd language using the rules of sounds of their first language, for example, when the L1 of Mandarin influences the production of L2 English.

Accents are most impacted by:
- **Phonology**: the speech sounds of languages (e.g., /g/ as in 'go', /s/ as in 'Sam')
- **Phonological Patterns**: rules for speech sounds in languages (e.g., in English, we have /ng/ in the medial and final position of words but not at the beginning of words, in other languages /ng/ at the beginning of words may be acceptable)
- **Prosody**: the rhythm of languages (e.g., syllable and word stress, rate of speech, intonation)

Dialects are most impacted by phonology in addition to:
- **Morphology**: rules for word formation (e.g., adjective vs. adverb)
- **Syntax**: grammatical rules
- **Semantics**: vocabulary
- **Pragmatics**: social norms for language use

The third layer to the discussion of accents and dialects is a term called idiolect. Idiolect refers to the speech habits that are unique to a particular person. No two idiolects are the same. Many personal and social factors that influence idiolects, especially now more than ever due to social media and television:

- Personality Preferences
- Geographical Location
- Family and Friends
- Outside Influences (e.g., celebrities, social media, role models)

Accent Modification (AM)

English is the 3rd most widely spoken language in the world, behind Chinese and Spanish (all dialects). There are approximately 160 dialects of English around the world. Even though English is not the most spoken language, it's considered the global business language, meaning most interactions and business transactions across countries are done in English.

However, there is no standard accent or dialect. Again, even within the U.S., there are 24 regional dialectal variations of American English. Those who seek accent modification services do so because their accent deviates from the native or standard accent of a community, and they perceive it to have negative consequences. Many clients choose to work on accent modification and professional speaking to improve their spoken English skills, raise self-awareness, or help work performance. After accent modification and professional speaking training, clients report benefits such as:

- Being more proficient communicators
- Increased confidence
- Gaining new professional skills

Improving one's accent is hard work and takes time. Unfortunately, these services are not covered by insurance and are often paid for out of pocket; therefore, most clients can only afford or have time for a few sessions. The resources in this book are intended to help professionals and clients quickly get started on working on accent modification and professional speaking. While there are several U.S. dialects, the most commonly sought-after one is General American English (GenAm). GenAm is an umbrella term for English speaking patterns that lack distinctive regional, ethnic, or socioeconomic characteristics. The topic areas and stimuli included in this book are based on strategies to improve the intelligibility and naturalness of GenAm, but the principles described can be applied to learning any accent or dialect.

Topic areas covered in this book include:
- **Segmentals**: consonants and vowels
- **Suprasegmentals**: rate of speech, intonation, syllable stress, word linking, volume, and resonance
- **Professional Speaking**: body language, grammar, small talk, phone effectiveness, and humor

In these areas, you will find explanations of each topic area, examples, and practice stimuli. There is a companion website that contains downloadable Word documents of the assessment materials and practice stimuli for you and your own clients. You can access the companion website at **https://GlobalSpeechTherapy.Com/AccentBook, see back cover for password**. Please abide by the terms of use for this book and companion materials.

American English is a tricky and funny language. Clients have lots of great questions about all the rules and exceptions. To keep the client on track, remind them that they learned their native language by listening. Have them focus on pronunciation, not the spelling of words or rules. The International Phonetic Alphabet (IPA) symbols may be helpful at times, but don't get bogged down with teaching the symbols. Other suggestions for clients to keep things moving is to remind them to:
- Keep practice conversations short
- Practice spontaneous speech as much as possible
- Practice with a variety of native speakers
- Listen to a variety of native speakers
- Find a partner to give feedback

Becoming a Native Speaker

Research shows that individuals who learn a language after the age of 12 will have a nonnative accent (Granena & Long, 2013).

Therefore, the patterns of their first language will influence their production of a second language, which is important to keep in mind for clients who come to you wanting to 'sound like a native speaker.' There are some exceptional learners, but this goal is likely unachievable for most. However, clients who focus on accent modification and professional speaking can become more effective speakers.

Actors and actresses who achieve native-sounding speech in shows and movies, such as Nicole Kidman and Hugh Laurie, are reading from a script that they have rehearsed many times with lots of coaching. Also, it's easier to learn a dialect of their language, such as British English or Australian English, than to learn a new language without a nonnative accent. Therefore, a British actor will have an easier time learning an American dialect for a role than an actor whose first language is not English. In spontaneous conversation and interviews, they often revert to their usual pronunciation patterns.

Spies also must work hard at their accents to blend in. They have better luck speaking with a dialect in a target country instead of learning the accent. For example, they may pretend to speak with an Irish dialect while living in the U.S. or have a cover for their accent, such as being born in the U.S. to parents who speak German. Most laypeople will hear an accent but will not be able to confirm whether the spy is accurately portraying that accent.

Cultural Competence

The American Speech-Language-Hearing Association (ASHA) defines cultural competence as *"understanding and appropriately responding to the unique combination of cultural variables and the full range of dimensions of diversity that the professional and client/patient/family bring to interactions"* (American Speech-Language-Hearing Association, n.d.).

It's important to understand your client's cultural background. There are helpful resources that describe culture, language, grammar, and phonetic inventories. Remember that these are meant to be a guide, not to describe each person's beliefs or attitudes from a given country. At the end of this subsection, there is a cultural competence checklist from ASHA.

Any accent modification service aims to help the client improve the confidence, intelligibility, and naturalness of a spoken language or dialect in social, academic, and professional settings. Clients should learn segmentals, or phonemes, used in General American English (GenAm) as well as suprasegmentals and cultural norms (e.g., eye contact, slang, humor, etc.). Accent modification services should be provided in a way that is respectful of the client and their cultural background.

Refer to the cultural competence checklist (Figure 2-2.) from ASHA on the next page for examples of cultural frameworks.

AMERICAN
SPEECH-LANGUAGE-
HEARING
ASSOCIATION

Cultural Competence Checklist: **Personal Reflection**

Ratings:
1 Strongly Agree
2 Agree
3 Neutral
4 Disagree
5 Strongly Disagree

This tool was developed to heighten your awareness of how you view clients/patients from culturally and linguistically diverse (CLD) populations.
*There is no answer key; however, you should review responses that you rated 5, 4, and even 3.

____ I treat all of my clients with respect for their culture.

____ I do not impose my beliefs and value systems on my clients, their family members, or their friends.

____ I believe that it is acceptable to use a language other than English in the U.S.

____ I accept my clients' decisions as to the degree to which they choose to acculturate into the dominant culture.

____ I provide services to clients who are GLBTQ (Gay, Lesbian, Bisexual, Transgender, or Questioning).

____ I am driven to respond to others' insensitive comments or behaviors.

____ I do not participate in insensitive comments or behaviors.

____ I am aware that the roles of family members may differ within or across culture or families.

____ I recognize family members and other designees as decision makers for services and support.

____ I respect non-traditional family structures (e.g., divorced parents, same gender parents, grandparents as caretakers).

____ I understand the difference between a communication disability and a communication difference.

____ I understand that views of the aging process may influence the clients'/families' decision to seek intervention.

____ I understand that there are several American English dialects. I recognize that all English speakers use a dialect of English.

I understand that the use of a foreign accent or limited English skill is not a reflection of:

____ Reduced intellectual capacity

____ The ability to communicate clearly and effectively in a native language

I understand how culture can affect child-rearing practices such as:

____ Discipline

____ Dressing

____ Toileting

____ Feeding

____ Self-help skills

____ Expectations for the future

____ Communication

I understand the impact of culture on life activities, such as:

____ Education

____ Family roles

____ Religion/faith-based practices

____ Gender roles

____ Alternative medicine

____ Customs or superstitions

____ Employment

____ Perception of time

____ Views of wellness

____ Views of disabilities

____ The value of Western medical treatment

I understand my clients' cultural norms may influence communication in many ways, including:

____ Eye contact

____ Interpersonal space

____ Use of gestures

____ Comfort with silence

____ Turn-taking

____ Topics of conversation

____ Asking and responding to questions

____ Greetings

____ Interruptions

____ Use of humor

____ Decision-making roles

---

*While several sources were consulted in the development of this checklist, the following document inspired its design:
Goode, T. D. (1989, revised 2002). Promoting cultural and linguistic competence self-assessment checklist for personnel
Providing services and supports in early intervention and childhood settings.

Reference this material as: American Speech-Language-Hearing Association. (2010). *Cultural Competence Checklist: Personal reflection.* Available
from www.asha.org/uploadedFiles/practice/multicultural/personalreflections.pdf.

© Copyright 2010 American Speech-Language-Hearing Association. All rights reserved.

Figure 2-2. Cultural Competence Checklist: Personal Reflection

Efficacy of Accent Modification

There are a lot of questions about the effectiveness of accent modification and the best techniques. Most of the research comes from TESOL (Teaching English as a Second or Foreign Language), but unfortunately, there still isn't much out there specific to accent modification or teaching pronunciation.

Let's first discuss what accent modification is and what it is not. Accent modification has many different titles that you may have heard, including:
- Accent Learning
- Accent Acquisition
- Pronunciation
- Accent or Dialect Coaching
- Accent or Dialect Training

It is okay to refer to accent modification services by any of these titles. There isn't one agreed upon title yet. It seems that most of the online searches by clients are for accent modification, English pronunciation, and accent reduction (even though the latter is an antiquated term). The overall goal for accent modification is accent congruence and helping clients achieve alignment with their accent and sense of self.

Above, I mention the benefits of accent modification and why people may seek it out. However, there are some negative connotations that the term accent modification, or any other related term, carries with it. This is for good reason; accent modification can be a very sensitive and personal topic. So, let's talk about what accent modification is NOT:
- Just articulation of sounds
- Accent reduction - you are teaching a new accent because there is no standard
- 'Americanizing' an accent or person
- Changing an identity

While clients may feel that others have a difficult time understanding their spoken English or may be referred by an employer or professor, most of the time, they are very interested in improving themselves. I can relate to this on a personal level! I have been learning Spanish for many years and have visited many Spanish-speaking countries. When I gather up my courage to practice Spanish in these countries with native speakers, it doesn't go well about half the time. Some listeners are very patient and work with me; others get confused and have no idea what I'm saying. It's frustrating for me, but I know I have much room for improvement with my Spanish-speaking skills. I cannot control the people with whom I interact. I can only improve myself so that hopefully, the next interaction goes more smoothly.

I do understand that others have different experiences and opinions. No one should ever feel forced to change themselves to meet others' expectations. Several factors impact the intelligibility of accents and dialects, and it's not all about the speaker's abilities:

- Listener's biases towards groups of people or accents
- Listener's familiarity with the topic
- Listener's familiarity with the L1 or dialect of the speaker
- Complexity of the topic

In summary, a listener's ability to understand accented speech depends on their familiarity with accented speech and the complexity of the topic (Jenson & Thøgersen, 2017).

Also, the expectation bias is true for both non-native speakers (NNS) and listeners. Non-native speakers may assume that they are asked to repeat themselves due to their accent, when in reality, native speakers have errors in their speech and are asked to repeat themselves at times, too. However, research does show that while native speakers have errors in their speech, it is more noticed in non-native speakers (Dalman & Kang, 2019).

Listeners may very well be biased against groups of people or accents and be completely unaware of this bias. For instance, white speakers are typically perceived to be from the United Kingdom, Australia, New Zealand, or the United States, and to be native English speakers. Listeners may even assume, based on someone's physical appearance or clothing, that they are from a non-English speaking country and assume they will have an accent. Therefore, they may perceive someone has an accent when they are a native English speaker.

So, what does this mean for clients? Listeners may give them inaccurate feedback about their accent, and non-native speakers may assume that typical miscommunications are due to their accent. It's important to remind clients that native speakers have communication mishaps as well. While listeners have a major role in the communication loop, we cannot work with every listener a non-native speaker will interact with. We can only work with clients and help them develop effective communication strategies based on their own needs and goals.

Core values of accent modification that I have found to be important combine self-development, client values, and professional development:

Self: Remain curious and open about cultures and experiences of others
Client: Develop effective communication strategies based on <u>own</u> needs
Profession: Demonstrate the unique strengths that disciplines bring to AM

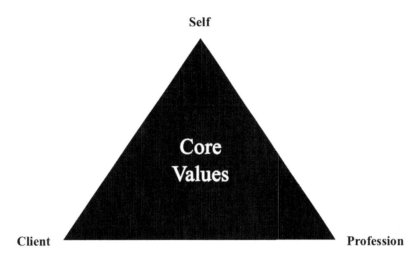

Figure 2-3. Core Values of Accent Modification

Principles of Accent Modification

Part of the reason for the lack of research specific to accent modification is that there is no standard language, accent, or dialect, making it difficult to obtain a baseline and measure outcomes. The goal of accent modification is to improve the intelligibility and naturalness of a spoken language or dialect, but that is very subjective. One might say that it's in the ears of the beholder. However, there are things known about speech development that can be applied to accent modification - like the core principles for accent modification, if you will.

1. **Phonological Awareness:** One factor in acquiring a new accent is phonological awareness. Phonological awareness refers to one's awareness of the phonological, or sound, structure of words and the ability to discriminate, remember, and manipulate sounds at the sentence, word, syllable, and phoneme (sound) level. Phonological awareness is important in accent modification because a client must be able to hear how sounds, syllables, and words are produced in isolation as well as connected speech. Clients must also be able to discriminate between variations in their own speech productions as well as others.

2. **Principles of Motor Learning (Motor Planning vs. Motor Adaptation):** Another factor in acquiring a new accent is motor learning. First, motor planning refers to the brain's ability to learn to perform steps to make movement happen (such

as walking, brushing your teeth, or speaking) and remember those steps. The more we perform a skill, the better we get at it. Specific to speech, we must first think about what to say, how to say it, and then execute those steps. Because of speech motor planning, the brain can automatically tell your mouth exactly how to say what you are thinking once you come up with a statement (and sometimes this occurs before you even realize what you are saying!). We don't have to remember how to produce every single sound to form a word or sentence.

We don't have to relearn how to speak every time we learn a new language, accent, or dialect, thanks to motor planning. We just need to adapt the skills we already have, which is referred to as motor adaptation. As a result, accent modification clients generally must focus on adapting their pronunciation of some consonants and vowels to make them more aspirated, longer, shorter, or adapt their prosody to match the rhythm of a language. In some cases, in which a L1 and L2 have different phonological repertoires, or sound inventories, a client may need to completely learn a new sound (Ojakangas, 2013).

Additionally, some clients have a true articulation, or speech sound disorder, that may have not been diagnosed earlier in their lives, such as a lisp or /w/ for /r/ substitution. In these cases, these clients must be referred to a Speech-Language Pathologist (SLP) for assessment and treatment.

Principles of motor learning tell us that new skills should be practiced in an easy context and then gradually made more challenging. Regarding accent modification, it's best first to teach a target and then address them individually in shorter utterances, followed by longer utterances.

I consider shorter utterances to be the introduction phase where these contexts are introduced and drilled:
a. Isolation/Syllables (phonemic sound level)
b. Single words
c. Phrases (2-4 combined words)

I consider longer utterances to be the carryover phase and consist of more complexity in these contexts:
a. Sentences (5+ combined words)
b. Reading passages aloud
c. Conversation

The following table shows conditions and their descriptions of the principles of motor learning that are relevant to accent modification.

Table 2-1. Conditions and Descriptions Principles of Motor Learning	
Condition	**Description**
Practice Amount	Small: Low number of practice trials (e.g., 10 trials)
	Large: High number of practice trials (e.g., 50 trials)
Practice Variability	Constant: Practice same target in same context (e.g., initial /s/ in words)
	Variable: Practice different targets in different contexts (e.g., initial, medial, final /s/ in words)
Practice Schedule	Blocked: Practice targets in successive blocks (e.g., one target per activity)
	Random: Practice is intermixed with other targets (e.g., addressing multiple targets per activity)
Feedback Frequency	High: After each trial
	Low: After several trials

Adapted from: (Maas et al., 2013).

In taking what is known about the speech principles of motor learning and applying them to accent modification, I think the following practice and feedback conditions are the most relevant.

Table 2-2. Practice Schedule Principles of Motor Learning	
Phase	**Principles of Motor Learning**
Introduction Phase (lots of drill): Isolation/Syllables Words Phrases	Practice Amount: Large Practice Variability: Constant Practice Schedule: Blocked Feedback Frequency: High
Carryover Phase: Sentences Reading Passages Aloud Conversation	Practice Amount: Small Practice Variability: Variable Practice Schedule: Random Feedback Frequency: Low

Adapted from: (Maas et al., 2013).

To help build the client's motor planning, motor adaptation, and phonological awareness skills, I use the following formats when addressing segmentals and suprasegmentals in short and long utterances. Remember the acronym **M.O.T.O.R.** Below is a description of each format and an example.

	Word	Description	Example for initial /s/
M	**Model**	Model the stimuli and have the client repeat after you	Instructor: "Say Sam" Client: "Sam"
O	**Opposites**	Have the client say the target and its opposite for negative practice	Instructor: "Say Sam, tham" Client: "Sam, tham"
T	**Tell apart**	Have the client distinguish between same/different productions for auditory discrimination	Instructor: "Which one is the target: Sam or tham" Client: "First one"
O	**Over-Correction**	Have the client say stimuli while over-emphasizing the target	Instructor: "Say Ssssam" Client: "Ssssam"
R	**Resay**	Have client say or read stimuli again independently in their natural voice	Client: "Sam"

Table 2-3. Formats for Practice

It's recommended to walk through each format for shorter utterances (isolation/syllables, words, phrases). For longer utterances (sentences, reading, spontaneous speech), choose 1-2 formats to use with the client. There are more suggestions for using these formats specific to each topic area throughout the book.

A client's ability to acquire a new accent or dialect depends on their ability to both hear the differences in sound production and the rhythm of the language as well as the ability to imitate those concepts. You may notice a trend in client progress as shown in Figure 2-4:

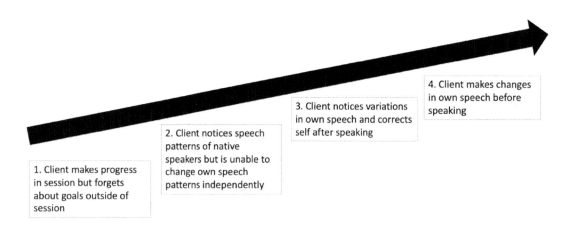

Figure 2-4. Client's Progress Graph

Who Works with Accents

Accent modification services are currently unregulated and offered by various professionals. Historically, English pronunciation has been done by English as Second Language (ESL) Teachers.

Professions have different approaches based on their training and skill set. Because of this, rates for accent modification can vary across disciplines, expertise, and geography. Many of these professions have their own organizations with resources. Some professions that work with accent include:

- ESL Teachers
- Foreign Language Teachers
- Voice Teachers/Coaches
- Acting Coaches
- Communication Instructors
- Applied Linguists
- Speech-Language Pathologists (SLPs)
- Speech-Language Pathologist Assistants (SLPAs)

SLPs bring many unique skills to the table, including:
- A clinical ear to hear sound production critically
- Knowing how to elicit target consonant and vowel sounds
- Understanding sound production in isolation through connected speech

A big question when getting started with accent modification is "How do I train my clinical ear?" It takes practice and time! There is no one way to describe characteristics of accents and dialects. As one becomes more exposed to sounds across accents and dialects, they will be able to dissect them more easily across languages. Listen to a variety of examples through TV, movies, websites, YouTube, radio, speaking partners, etc. Don't focus so much on professional terminology; instead, ask yourself "How would I describe this to myself?" It also helps to imitate what you hear and to watch your client's mouth. You won't just hear variations in sound production - you will see it through jaw height, lip roundedness, and tongue placement. Remember to bring your critical ear; if something sounds different, it probably is.

Along with hearing accents, professionals often wonder about their own speaking patterns and their ability to model or imitate accents. The short answer is that there are so many different accents, dialects, and idiolects in the world that it is impossible for one to learn them all and produce them like a native speaker. So no, you don't need to be able to model a particular pattern or accent to teach it. Just use audio examples from the internet such as YouTube, Wikipedia, Google, etc.!

Before getting started with coaching sessions, gather client background information, their goals, and develop a plan. To do those things, a recommended assessment and screener are included in the next section.

References

American Speech-Language-Hearing Association (n.d.). *Accent Modification* (Practice Portal). Retrieved March 14, 2022. from www.asha.org/Practice-Portal/Professional-Issues/Accent-Modification/.

American Speech-Language-Hearing Association (n.d.). *Cultural Competence.* (Practice Portal). Retrieved December 1, 2021. from www.asha.org/Practice-Portal/Professional-Issues/Cultural-Competence/.

Dalman, M., & Kang, O. (2019). Listener background in L2 speech evaluation. *Metacognition in Learning.* https://doi.org/10.5772/intechopen.89414

Delaney, R. (2013). *Dialect map of American English* [Infographic]. Robertspage.com. http://robertspage.com/dialects.html.

Granena G, Long MH. Age of onset, length of residence, language aptitude, and ultimate L2 attainment in three linguistic domains. *Second Language Research.* 2013;29(3):311–343.

Jensen, Christian and Jacob Thøgersen. Foreign accent, cognitive load, and intelligibility of EMI lectures. *Nordic Journal of English Studies.* 2017;16(3):107-137.

Maas, E., Robin, D. A., Austermann Hula, S. N., Freedman, S. E., Wulf, G., Ballard, K. J., & Schmidt, R. A. (2008). Principles of motor learning in treatment of motor speech disorders. American Journal of Speech-Language Pathology, 17, 277–298.

Ojakangas, C. L. (2013). Viewpoint: What brain research can tell us about accent modification. *Perspectives on Communication Disorders and Sciences in Culturally and Linguistically Diverse (CLD) Populations, 20*(3), 101–108. https://doi.org/10.1044/cds20.3.101

Section

3

Assessment

Since several factors influence an accent, it's important to learn as much as possible about the client's language development, personal goals, and speaking patterns. Below are resources to use for an assessment. This tool is not a standardized assessment, meaning it does not compare the client's skills to those of other non-native speakers. Not all clients will want/need an assessment. If that is the case, there is a screener that takes about 10 minutes, or you can jump to the topic areas and get started.

Assessment Areas

A. **Case History:** A questionnaire to be completed with the client to gather more information about their language background, use, and concerns

B. **Hearing Screening Form:** A questionnaire to be completed with the client to gather more information about their hearing health

C. **Oral Peripheral Exam:** An observational tool that looks at the strength, range of motion, coordination, and appearance of articulators for speech production

D. **Instructor Packet:** Sections for instructors to complete during the assessment

Section 1. *Articulation of Consonants and Vowels:* Rates the client's productions of consonants and vowels in GenAm in all word positions of words, phrases, and sentences

Section 2. *Intonation:* Rates the client's perception and production of rising and falling intonation to indicate message meaning

Section 3. *Syllable Stress:* Rates the client's use of prosodic features to stress the main syllable in a word with two or more syllables

Section 4. *Word Linking in Sentences:* Rates the client's ability to link the end of a word to the beginning of another

Section 5. *Auditory Discrimination:* Rates the client's ability to discriminate between sounds in words and sentences as same or different

Section 6. *Reading Passage:* Rates the client's sound production in structured, connected speech

Section 7. *Spontaneous Speech Sample:* An observational tool that rates the client's sound production, language use, and pragmatics in spontaneous, connected speech

E. **Client Packet:** Stimuli for the client to read during the assessment

F. **Functional Communication Inventory (FCI):** A questionnaire for the client to complete based on their everyday routines

G. **Assessment Report Template:** A template for writing up assessment findings

H. **Goal Bank:** Suggested goals for each topic area addressed

I. **Assessment Report Example:** An example of a completed assessment report

Case History Form

Instructor

Instructor's name: _____ Today's date: _____

Client Contact Information

Client's full name: _____

Preferred name: _____ Preferred pronoun(s): _____

Address: _____

Email address: _____ Phone number: _____

Background Information

Date of birth: _____ Native country: _____

How long in U.S.: _____ years _____ months

Native language(s) spoken: _____

Where and when did you learn English: _____

Were your instructors native English speakers: ☐ Yes ☐ No

Number of years you have spoken English: _____

Additional languages you speak: _____

Do you have a history of speech or language problems in your native language:
☐ Yes ☐ No

General

Percentage of time you speak English on a typical weekday: ____ weekend: ____

Do you feel that people have difficulty understanding your spoken English:
☐ Yes ☐ No

If yes, describe: _____

Current employer: _____

List responsibilities: _____

Are you in school: ☐ Yes ☐ No If yes, what year/program: _____

What areas do you have difficulty with (check all that are applicable):

_____ Pronouncing speech sounds such as _____

_____ Being understood in social interactions

_____ Understanding social interactions

_____ Using and understanding idioms/slang

_____ Being understood in professional situations

_____ Understanding others in professional situations

_____ Grammar

_____ Other: _____

Has your accent impacted any of the following (check all that are applicable):

_____ Academic advancement	_____ Career advancement
_____ Professional interactions	_____ Social interactions
_____ Public speaking situations	_____ Telephone conversations
_____ Other: _____	

Do you have concerns about your hearing: ☐ Yes ☐ No

Do you have concerns about your vision: ☐ Yes ☐ No

Hearing Screening Form

Do you have a history of middle ear disease? ☐ Yes ☐ No

If yes, describe: _____

Have you had ear surgery? ☐ Yes ☐ No

If yes, describe: _____

Do you have a family history of hearing loss? ☐ Yes ☐ No

If yes, who and when diagnosed? _____

Do you have a history of any chronic loud noise exposure? ☐ Yes ☐ No

If yes, describe: _____

If you have access to an audiometer or other hearing screening instrument, you can complete a hearing screening. Expected results can be found below.

Right Ear		
1000	**2000**	**4000**

Left Ear		
1000	**2000**	**4000**

Results

☐ 1. Pass

☐ 2. Fail: Retest

☐ 3. Fail: Refer to Audiologist or ENT

Oral Peripheral Exam

The oral peripheral examination evaluates the structure and function of the speech mechanism to assess whether the system is adequate for speech production and should be completed by a Speech-Language Pathologist or other professionals with the appropriate training. Materials suggested: pen, light, timer, gloves, and tongue depressor.

*WNL = Within Normal Limits

FACE	WNL	Observations	
Appearance:			
Overall	☐	☐ Wide	☐ Narrow
Facial Symmetry	☐	☐ Asymmetrical features	
Spacing of Eyes	☐	☐ Wide	☐ Narrow
Head Size	☐	☐ Large	☐ Small
Tone	☐	☐ Hypertonic	☐ Hypotonic
Facial Expressions	☐	☐ Flat Affect	☐ Labile
Notes/Effect on speech:			

JAW	WNL	Observations
Coordination:		
Open and close jaw 2x	☐	☐ Reduced
Strength:		
Open and close jaw 2x w/resistance	☐	☐ Reduced
Notes/Effect on speech:		

LIPS	WNL	Observations	
Appearance:			
Posture at rest	N/A	☐ Closed	☐ Open
Drooling	N/A	☐ No	☐ Yes
Range of Motion:			
Retraction (smile)	☐	☐ Reduced right / left side	
Protrusion (pucker)	☐	☐ Reduced right / left side	
Coordination:			
Produce /u/➔/i/ 3x	☐	☐ Reduced	
Strength:			
Lip pop	☐	☐ Reduced	
Hold cheek puff for > 3 sec.	☐	☐ Reduced (seconds held: _____)	
Notes/Effect on speech:			

TEETH	WNL	Observations		
Appearance:				
Occlusion	☐	☐ Overbite	☐ Underbite	☐ Open bite
Hygiene	☐	☐ Concerns:		
Notes/Effect on speech:				

TONGUE	WNL	Observations
Appearance:		
Excursion	☐	☐ Deviates right / left side
Size	☐	☐ Large ☐ Small
Frenulum	☐	☐ Long
Range of Motion:		
Internal elevation	☐	☐ Reduced
Internal depression	☐	☐ Reduced
Internal lateralization	☐	☐ Reduced
External elevation	☐	☐ Reduced
External depression	☐	☐ Reduced
External lateralization	☐	☐ Reduced
Coordination:		
Rapid side to side 3x	☐	☐ Reduced
Circle around lips 2x	☐	☐ Reduced
Strength:		
Excursion w/ resistance	☐	☐ Reduced
Elevation w/ resistance	☐	☐ Reduced
Depression w/ resistance	☐	☐ Reduced
Lateralization w/ resistance	☐	☐ Reduced
Notes/Effect on speech:		

HARD PALATE	WNL	Observations	
Appearance:			
Overall	☐	☐ Clefting	☐ Growths
Color	☐	☐ Other (describe: _____)	
Height	☐	☐ High	☐ Short
Width	☐	☐ Wide	☐ Narrow
Length	☐	☐ Long	☐ Short
Symmetry	☐	☐ Asymmetrical	
Notes/Effect on speech:			

SOFT PALATE	WNL	Observations	
Appearance:			
Overall	☐	☐ Clefting	☐ Growths
Color	☐	☐ Other (describe: _____)	
Height	☐	☐ High	☐ Short
Width	☐	☐ Wide	☐ Narrow
Length	☐	☐ Long	☐ Short
Symmetry	☐	☐ Asymmetrical	
Tonsils	☐	☐ Large	☐ Removed
Notes/Effect on speech:			

VOICE	WNL	Observations	
Breath Support:			
Sustained 'ah' for 14+ seconds	☐	☐ Decreased (seconds held: _____)	
Sustained 's' for 20+ seconds	☐	☐ Decreased (seconds held: _____)	
Sustained 'z' for 20+ seconds	☐	☐ Decreased (seconds held: _____)	
Characteristics:			
Resonance	☐	☐ Hypernasal	☐ Hyponasal
Pitch	☐	☐ High	☐ Low
Quality	☐	☐ Raspy/Harsh	☐ Breathy
Volume	☐	☐ Loud	☐ Soft
Notes/Effect on speech:			

DIADOCHOKINETCIC RATES (DDK)	WNL	Observations
Not assessed before 6 years of age		
Directions: Tell client "Say target as many times as possible until I say 'stop."		
Succession: norm is 25-35 repetitions in 5 seconds		
Target: pʌ	☐	☐ Decreased (seconds held: _____)
Target: tʌ	☐	☐ Decreased (seconds held: _____)
Target: kʌ	☐	☐ Decreased (seconds held: _____)
Alternating: norm is 13-37 repetitions in 5 seconds		
Target: pʌtʌkʌ		☐ Decreased (seconds held: _____)
Notes/Effect on speech:		

Instructor Packet

The initial assessment evaluates the client's segmental and suprasegmental productions. Each subtest includes instructions, instructor stimuli, places to score, and places to make notes. A corresponding *Client Packet* is available for the client to reference during the assessment. Subtests that have client stimuli are noted in the instructions.

Section 1. *Articulation of Consonants and Vowels:* Rates client's productions of consonants and vowels in GenAm in all positions of words, phrases, and sentences

Section 2. *Intonation:* Rates the client's perception and production of rising and falling of intonation to indicate message meaning

Section 3. *Syllable Stress:* Rates the client's use of prosodic features to stress the main syllable in a word with two or more syllables

Section 4. *Word Linking in Sentences:* Rates client's ability to link the end of a word to the beginning of another

Section 5. *Auditory Discrimination:* Rates client's ability to discriminate between sounds in words and sentences as same or different

Section 6. *Reading Passage:* Rates client's sound production in structured, connected speech

Section 7. *Spontaneous Speech Sample:* Rates client's sound production, language use, and pragmatics in spontaneous, connected speech

Section 1. Articulation of Consonants and Vowels

Instruction: To the client say, "Please read the words presented. Speak in your natural voice."

Note – Corresponds to section 2 of the Client Packet. The words with the target sounds are bolded. There is extra space to note the client's productions. A diacritic chart is included to help you describe variations. Only the most common consonants produced with variation and those that impact intelligibility are included to save time.

Diacritic Chart			
Meaning	**Diacritic**	**Meaning**	**Diacritic**
Devoiced	m̥	Voiced	m̬
More Rounded	ǫ	Less Rounded	o̜
Extra short	ã	Lengthened	u:
Unaspirated	p=	Aspirated	pʰ

1. /t/

a	**Too**	Black **tie**	The **table** is already set
b	**Utensil**	Big **military**	*This **Saturday** is a holiday
c	*****Eat**	*****Not** now	*The **cat** woke me up

*Should be substituted as a /d/ or glottal stop

2. /d/

a	**Do**	Pizza **dough**	Wipe all the **dust** off
b	**Lady**	Loud **radio**	We have chocolate **pudding** too
c	*****Add**	*****Odd** couple	*The fire needs more **wood**

*Should be substituted as a very light /d/ or glottal stop

3. /s/

a	**See**	Hot **sun**	Read the **sign** before parking
b	**Listen**	Sore **muscle**	I left him a **message**
c	**Ice**	**Nice** job	We have **class** on Monday

4. /z/

a	**Zoo**	**Zach** left	What is the **zip** code
b	**Fuzzy**	Two **dozen**	He gave me a **present**
c	**Nose**	Honey **bees**	I lost my **keys** yesterday

5. /f/

a	**Fee**	Crisp **fall**	The **fan** is on high
b	**Office**	Cold **coffee**	I lost my **headphones** today
c	**Off**	Good **stuff**	Please just give me **half**

6. /v/

a	**Van**	Grape **vine**	The glass **vase** just broke
b	**Seven**	**Heavy** box	I don't like brown **gravy**
c	**Love**	**Move** here	The big **wave** crashed down

7. /θ/

a	**Thin**	**Think** again	**Thank** you for being here
b	**Python**	An **author**	Leave **nothing** in your pockets
c	**With**	Brown **moth**	Brush your **teeth** every night

8. /ɹ/

a	**Run**	Fast **race**	I saw a white **rabbit**
b	**Pirate**	Tooth **fairy**	The **arrow** is pointing south
c	**Four**	Blue **car**	Don't sit in the **chair**

9. /l/

a	**Lie**	**Long** day	Use the **ladder** out back
b	**Wallet**	D.C. **police**	The **polar** bear is sleeping
c	**All**	Sharp **tool**	Please **call** your parents now

10. /n/

a	No	Not here	I heard a loud knock
b	Any	Small pony	When will dinner be ready
c	On	Sticky bun	My ice cream cone melted

11. /ʃ/

a	Chef	Shy girl	We had to shop today
b	Lotion	Soft cushion	The fax machine is broken
c	Cash	Wash hands	He paid in cash too

12. /tʃ/

a	Chat	Chew gum	There is an autumn chill
b	Kitchen	Key chain	The new pitcher is great
c	Touch	Red couch	My watch stopped just now

13. /dʒ/

a	Jam	Close jar	Jet blue has good deals
b	Pigeon	It's magic	The edges are very sharp
c	Age	Huge spider	What page is it on

14. /ʒ/

a	Asia	My vision	She is usually working late
b	Beige	Ice luge	The new pants are camouflage

15. /w/

a	Wide	Big wind	The web is back again
b	Kiwi	My award	I left the microwave going

16. /h/

a	He	Hop off	The door pinched my hand
b	Beehive	In Ohio	They must behave or leave

17. Blends

a	**Prize**	Big **prey**	He is full of **pride**
b	**Clay**	Nice **clown**	**Close** the door right now
c	**Smoke**	Bad **smell**	The **smog** is very thick

18. Vowels

a	/i/	**Eat**	**Real cheap**	The **peach seemed sweet**
b	/ɪ/	**Is**	**Did win**	The **thick quilt** has a **stitch**
c	/e/	**Say**	**Came late**	The **gray cape** has a **label**
d	/ɛ/	**Egg**	**Ten cents**	The **eggshell** is in the **bread**
e	/æ/	**App**	**Grab bag**	The **van has** a **flat** tire
f	/ʌ/	**Up**	**Much trust**	**Brush** the **crust** with **butter**
g	/u/	**Food**	**Too soon**	**Move** the **two** bar **stools**
h	/ʊ/	**Good**	**Look good**	The **book nook looks good**
i	/o/	**Oat**	**Wrote note**	I **vote** for **goat yoga**
j	/a/	**Off**	**Lock dock**	**Blot** the **spot** with the **mop**
k	/ɔ/	**Ought**	**Long song**	Play **fall ball** on the **lawn**
l	/aɪ/	**Ice**	**I've tried**	The **dried spice** is **nice**
m	/aʊ/	**Ow**	**Browse town**	The **crowd** is **shouting loudly**
n	/ɔɪ/	**Oil**	**Oiled joints**	The **employee voiced** his **joys**

Section 2. Intonation

Note - There are no client stimuli for this section.

3.1 **Perception**

Instruction: To the client say, "Intonation refers to the rising and falling pitch of the voice in speaking to convey meaning. Listen to the following sentences and tell me if I use a rising or falling intonation."

Note- Read the sentences aloud using a typical intonation according to the cue in parentheses. The intended meaning is also in parentheses. There are 5 sentences in each subsection, 10 in total.

(make a list, falling) We need chocolate, sugar, and butter.
(clarification, rising) Are you applying to George Washington University, too?
(yes/no question, rising) Did you see the parade yesterday?
(statement, falling) This week is very busy.
(unfinished thought, rising) I may go to the movies, but….

Note- Read the sentences aloud using an atypical intonation according to the cue in parentheses. The intended meaning is also in parentheses. There are 5 sentences in each subsection, 10 in total.

(statement, rising) Today is a busy day.
(final comment, rising) I think I saw him after the movie on Friday.
(tag question, falling) We need napkins, plates, and spoons, right?
(statement, rising) I went to the store today.
(clarification, falling) Did you say you like cats?

Perception Total: / 10

3.2 **Production**

Instruction: To the client say, "I'm going to ask you a question. Please respond using a full sentence using your natural voice."

Note - The prompts are a guide. Do your best to consider the client's intonation pattern in their response to the conversational topic and determine if it sounds natural or unnatural. There are 5 questions in total.

1. On Saturday, we need to bring chips, salsa, and cheese to the party. What 3 things do we need to bring?

   Client should repeat the list using falling intonation

2. What day of the week is today?

   Client should answer with a falling intonation

3. What would you ask a friend who just got back from a trip?

   If yes/no question (e.g., "Did you have fun"), then client should use rising intonation

   If what, where, who, when, or why question (e.g., "What did you do on your trip"), then client should use falling intonation

4. I like tea with cream and sugar. How would you confirm that fact with me if you were ordering a drink for me?

   Client should answer with a question using rising intonation

5. How would you tell a stranger, "The train is one block on the left" if you are unsure of yourself?

   Client should answer using rising intonation

Production Total: / 5

Section 3. Syllable Stress

Instruction: To the client say, "Please read each sentence aloud. Pause after reading the sentence until I am ready for you to continue. Remember to speak in your natural voice."

*Note – Corresponds to section 4 of the Client Packet. The target word is <u>underlined</u>, and the stressed syllable is **bolded**. There are 10 words in total.*

1. You need to <u>in**sert**</u> the credit card into the machine

2. I didn't <u>ob**ject**</u> to the vote

3. He gave me a <u>**pre**sent</u> for my birthday

4. Trader Joe's gets fresh <u>**pro**duce</u> every Wednesday

5. For the <u>**re**cord</u>, Glen Lake is 50 feet deep

6. We could not get a <u>**per**mit</u> for the march

7. The <u>pho**tog**rapher</u> is well-traveled and world-famous

8. I really like <u>pho**tog**raphy</u> and running

9. I am <u>ad**dict**ed</u> to caffeine and sugar

10. I need to do more <u>re**search**</u> for my paper that is due Monday

Total: _____ / 10

Section 4. Word Linking in Sentences

Instruction: To the client say, "Please read each sentence aloud. Pause after stating the sentence until I am ready for you to continue. Remember to speak in your natural voice."

Note – Corresponds to section 5 of the Client Packet. Words that should be linked are noted with (-). There are 20 links in total.

1. We need-a new start-time

2. He bought-a new-water toy

3. I finished the-apple for my snack

4. The college-is-in Washington, D.C.

5. Where's the market

6. What's your favorite-time-of year

7. We will go-on-a hike later today

8. I have-a big-game coming-up

9. We will-leave-at 11-05 sharp

10. I sat-in the middle-of the-row

Total: / 20

Section 5. Auditory Discrimination

Note - There are no client stimuli for this section. Remember to cover your mouth during this portion!

6.1 **Words**

Instruction: To the client say, "I'm going to say two words, one right after the other. Tell me whether these two words are the same or different. I cannot repeat."

1. grade/grade (same)
2. bad/bat (different)
3. past/past (same)
4. sack/sock (different)
5. yes/yes (same)
6. not/note (different)
7. laws/loss (different)
8. could/could (same)
9. shine/shine (same)
10. weak/wake (different)
11. heat/hit (different)
12. cup/cop (different)
13. played/played (same)
14. fall/fault (different)
15. sick/sick (same)

Words Total: / 15

6.2 **Sentences**

Instruction: To the client say, "I'm going to say two sentences, one right after the other. Tell me whether these two sentences are the same or different. I cannot repeat."

1. We have more bags / We have more bugs (different)
2. He's a lap dog / He's a lab dog (different)
3. I need a cup / I need a cup (same)
4. The boat is in the wave / The boat is in the wake (different)
5. The big guys are watching you / The big guys are watching you (same)

Sentences Total: / 5

Section 6. Reading Passage

Instruction: To the client say, "When I say '*Start*', please read the given reading passage in your natural voice."

Note - Corresponds to section 7 of the Client Packet. Use a stopwatch to record the time it takes for the client to read the passage. (Slow = more than 1 minute, 38 seconds; Average = 1 minute, 27 seconds; Fast = less than 1 minute, 18 seconds)

The Caterpillar

Do you like amusement parks? Well, I sure do. To amuse myself, I went twice last spring. My most memorable moment was riding on the Caterpillar, which is a gigantic roller coaster high above the ground. When I saw how high the Caterpillar rose into the bright blue sky, I knew it was for me. After waiting in line for thirty minutes, I made it to the front where the man measured my height to see if I was tall enough. I gave the man my coins, asked for change, and jumped on the cart. Tick, tick, tick, the Caterpillar climbed slowly up the tracks. It went so high I could see the parking lot. Boy, was I scared! I thought to myself, "There's no turning back now." People were so scared they screamed as we swiftly zoomed fast, fast, and faster along the tracks. As quickly as it started, the Caterpillar came to a stop. Unfortunately, it was time to pack the car and drive home. That night I dreamt of the wild ride on the Caterpillar. Taking a trip to the amusement park and riding on the Caterpillar was my most memorable moment ever! (Patel et al., 2013).

(196 words)

Rate Total: _____ Minute _____ Seconds

Section 7. Spontaneous Speech Sample

Instruction: To the client say, "Now I'd like for you to talk for 2-3 minutes. I will time you. You can talk about your field of study or job, hobbies or interests, or any other topic. Remember to use your natural voice."

Other prompts: favorite meal to cook, compare local city to their home city, favorite holiday tradition.

Note - There are no client stimuli for this section. Listen to the client speak for 2-3 minutes and note any productions you hear that impact intelligibility or naturalness.

Consonant variations noted in conversation

Vowel variations noted in conversation

Grammatical difficulties noted in conversation

Overall intelligibility judged to be
☐ 1. Highly unintelligible
☐ 2. Intelligible in a known context
☐ 3. Distinct accent but intelligible
☐ 4. Intelligible with some trace of an accent
☐ 5. Nearly native

Voice and rate of speech in conversation	
Rate of Speech ☐ 1. Slow ☐ 2. Natural rate ☐ 3. Fast	Volume ☐ 1. Soft ☐ 2. Natural volume ☐ 3. Loud
Vocal Quality ☐ Within Normal Limits ☐ Raspy ☐ Harsh ☐ Breathy ☐ Other	Vocal Resonance ☐ Oral ☐ Pharyngeal ☐ Nasal

Pragmatics	
Eye Contact ☐ Within Normal Limits ☐ Too Much ☐ Too Little	Distance Between Speakers ☐ Within Normal Limits ☐ Too close ☐ Too far
Topic Maintenance ☐ Within Normal Limits ☐ Tangential ☐ Limited or vague utterances	Gestures ☐ Not distracting ☐ Too much, very distracting ☐ No gestures
Turn-Taking ☐ Within Normal Limits ☐ Interruptions ☐ Limited or vague utterances	Facial Expressions ☐ Within Normal Limits ☐ Ambiguous ☐ Mismatch
Use of Humor ☐ Appropriate ☐ Inappropriate (describe):	Demeanor ☐ Pleasant, friendly ☐ Other (describe):

Notes

<u>Client Packet</u>

<u>Client instructions:</u> You have stimuli for only the sections that you need (no client stimuli for sections 3, 6, or 8). Wait for the Instructor to give you instructions for each subtest.

Section 1. Articulation of Consonants and Vowels
Section 2. No client stimuli
Section 3. Syllable Stress
Section 4. Word Linking in Sentences
Section 5. No client stimuli
Section 6. Reading Passage
Section 7. No client stimuli

Section 1. Articulation of Consonants and Vowels

1.

a	Too	Black tie	The table is already set
b	Utensil	Big military	This Saturday is a holiday
c	Eat	Not now	The cat woke me up

2.

a	Do	Pizza dough	Wipe all the dust off
b	Lady	Loud radio	We have chocolate pudding too
c	Add	Odd couple	The fire needs more wood

3.

a	See	Hot sun	Read the sign before parking
b	Listen	Sore muscle	I left him a message
c	Ice	Nice job	We have class on Monday

4.

a	Zoo	Zach left	What is the zip code
b	Fuzzy	Two dozen	He gave me a present
c	Nose	Honey bees	I lost my keys yesterday

5.

a	Fee	Crisp fall	The fan is on high
b	Office	Cold coffee	I lost my headphones today
c	Off	Good stuff	Please just give me half

6.

a	Van	Grape vine	The glass vase just broke
b	Seven	Heavy box	I don't like brown gravy
c	Love	Move here	The big wave crashed down

7.

a	Thin	Think again	Thank you for being here
b	Python	An author	Leave nothing in your pockets
c	With	Brown moth	Brush your teeth every night

8.

a	Run	Fast race	I saw a white rabbit
b	Pirate	Tooth fairy	The arrow is pointing south
c	Four	Blue car	Don't sit in the chair

9.

a	Lie	Long day	Use the ladder out back
b	Wallet	DC police	The polar bear is sleeping
c	All	Sharp tool	Please call your parents now

10.

a	No	Not here	I heard a loud knock
b	Any	Small pony	When will dinner be ready
c	On	Sticky bun	My ice cream cone melted

11.

a	Chef	Shy girl	We had to shop today
b	Lotion	Soft cushion	The fax machine is broken
c	Cash	Wash hands	He paid in cash too

12.

a	Chat	Chew gum	There is an autumn chill
b	Kitchen	Key chain	The new pitcher is great
c	Touch	Red couch	My watch stopped just now

13.

a	Jam	Close jar	Jet blue has good deals
b	Pigeon	It's magic	The edges are very sharp
c	Age	Huge spider	What page is it on

14.

a	Asia	My vision	She is usually working late
b	Beige	Ice luge	The new pants are camouflage

15.

a	Wide	Big wind	The web is back again
b	Kiwi	My award	I left the microwave going

16.

a	He	Hop off	The door pinched my hand
b	Beehive	In Ohio	They must behave or leave

17.

a	Prize	Big prey	He is full of pride
b	Clay	Nice clown	Close the door right now
c	Smoke	Bad smell	The smog is very thick

18.

a	Eat	Real cheap	The peach seemed sweet
b	Is	Did win	The thick quilt has a stitch
c	Say	Came late	The gray cape has a label
d	Egg	Ten cents	The eggshell is in the bread
e	App	Grab bag	The van has a flat tire
f	Up	Much trust	Brush the crust with butter
g	Food	Too soon	Move the two bar stools
h	Good	Look good	The book nook looks good
i	Oat	Wrote note	I vote for goat yoga
j	Off	Lock dock	Blot the spot with the mop
k	Ought	Long song	Play fall ball on the lawn
l	Ice	I've tried	The dried spice is nice
m	Ow	Browse town	The crowd is shouting loudly
n	Oil	Oiled joints	The employee voiced his joys

Section 3. Syllable Stress

1. You need to insert the credit card into the machine

2. I didn't object to the vote

3. He gave me a present for my birthday

4. Trader Joe's gets fresh produce every Wednesday

5. For the record, Glen Lake is 50 feet deep

6. We could not get a permit for the march

7. The photographer is well-traveled and world-famous

8. I really like photography and running

9. I am addicted to caffeine and sugar

10. I need to do more research for my paper that is due Monday

Section 4. Word Linking in Sentences

1. We need a new start time

2. He bought a new water toy

3. I finished the apple for my snack

4. The college is in Washington, D.C.

5. Where's the market

6. What's your favorite time of year

7. We will go on a hike later today

8. I have a big game coming up

9. We will leave at 11:05 sharp

10. I sat in the middle of the row

Section 6. Reading Passage

The Caterpillar

Do you like amusement parks? Well, I sure do. To amuse myself, I went twice last spring. My most memorable moment was riding on the Caterpillar, which is a gigantic roller coaster high above the ground. When I saw how high the Caterpillar rose into the bright blue sky, I knew it was for me. After waiting in line for thirty minutes, I made it to the front where the man measured my height to see if I was tall enough. I gave the man my coins, asked for change, and jumped on the cart. Tick, tick, tick, the Caterpillar climbed slowly up the tracks. It went so high I could see the parking lot. Boy, was I scared! I thought to myself, "There's no turning back now." People were so scared they screamed as we swiftly zoomed fast, fast, and faster along the tracks. As quickly as it started, the Caterpillar came to a stop. Unfortunately, it was time to pack the car and drive home. That night I dreamt of the wild ride on the Caterpillar. Taking a trip to the amusement park and riding on the Caterpillar was my most memorable moment ever! (Patel et al., 2013).

Functional Communication Inventory (FCI)

Below are topics and questions to better understand your client and incorporate targeted stimuli that aligns with their everyday life.

Instruction: Ask your client the questions below and document their responses to customize future sessions and practice assignments. The more client-tailored and applicable the stimuli, the greater the probability of the impact the sessions and practice will have. It is recommended that you begin this section during the assessment and then send home the FCI with the client to continue working on.

Self-Reflection: Who do you admire as a speaker? How would you describe their speech?

Relevant information for future sessions and homework:

1. What hobbies/interests do you have?

2. What are your preferred sources for current events?

3. What types of articles/publications are of most interest to you?

4. Write your typical voicemail message:

5. List 5-10 common statements or questions you use in your work environment:
   (e.g., I will be late; My internet is not working)

6. List 5-10 common statements or questions you use in your academic environment:
   (e.g., I need help with algebra; I don't understand biology and physics)

7. List 5-10 common statements or questions you use in your social environment:
   (e.g., Will you meet me at the grocery store; Do you want to meet up for dinner and drinks)

8. Other

Accent Modification and Professional Speaking Assessment Report			
Client Name:		Preferred Name:	
Pronouns:		Date of Birth:	
Phone No:		Email Address:	
Mailing Address:			
Evaluator:		Date of Report:	

REASON FOR REFERRAL

<Client Name> was <self-referred / referred by (Name), (state title) > for accent modification services. <Client Name> reported that <he/she/they> has difficulty with <include areas noted in case history> and that this has negatively impacted <his/her/their> <include areas from case history>.

BACKGROUND INFORMATION

<Client Name> is a <male/female/non-binary> adult from <country>. <Client Name>'s native language is <state native language/s>. <Client Name> has lived in the U.S. for < # > years and < # > months. <Client Name> has been speaking English for < # > years. <Client Name> learned English <state how and when> and <his/her/their> instructors <were/were not> native English speakers. <Client Name> is also fluent in <state other languages fluent in, other than English and native language>.

<Client Name> currently works at <state where the client currently works and position>

OR

<Client Name> is currently in school <state school name, what level of study, area of study>. <Client Name> reported that <he/she/they> uses English < # >% of the time during the week and < # >% of the time on the weekends. <Client Name> <has/has not> received accent modification services previously and <does/does not> report a history of speech or language disorder in <his/her/their> native language. <If the client has received accent modification services or has a history of speech or language disorder, include details>.

ASSESSMENTS AND RESULTS

The following tools were administered in English on <state date>:
1. Hearing Screening
2. Oral Mechanism Exam
3. Non-Standardized Assessment

The following areas of General American English (GenAm) were assessed:
a. Articulation
b. Intonation
c. Syllable Stress
d. Word Linking in Sentences
e. Auditory Discrimination
f. Rate of Speech

The assessment description and results are as follows:

1. Hearing Screening
<Client Name>'s hearing was screened in both the right and the left ears at 25 dB at 500 Hz, 1000 Hz, 2000 Hz, and 4000 Hz. <Client Name> <passed/did not pass> across all frequencies in both ears. <Client Name> reported that <he/she/they> <did/did not> have concerns regarding <his/her/their> hearing. <If client has concerns with hearing, include details:>

2. Oral Mechanism Examination
An oral mechanism examination was administered to evaluate the structural and functional integrity of <Client Name>'s oral mechanism for speech production. Results are as follows:

Face: Overall appearance, symmetry, and tone appear to be within normal limits
    OR <Describe characteristics>
Jaw: Range of motion and strength appear to be within normal limits
    OR <Describe characteristics>
Lips: Range of motion, coordination, and strength appear to be within normal limits
    OR <Describe characteristics>
Teeth: Occlusion and structure appear to be within normal limits
    OR <Describe characteristics>
Tongue: Range of motion, coordination, and strength appear to be within normal limits
    OR <Describe characteristics>
Hard Palate: Structure and symmetry appear to be within normal limits

OR <Describe characteristics>

Soft Palate: Structure, symmetry, and mobility appear to be within normal limits

OR <Describe characteristics>

Diadochokinesis (DDK): <Client Name>'s ability to coordinate production of syllables in rapid succession (e.g., "papapapa") and rapidly alternate speech movements (e.g., "pataka") is within normal limits

OR <Describe characteristics>

3. Non-Standardized Assessment
*WNL = Within Normal Limits

a.   Articulation: Refers to the production of sounds in the GenAm phonemic repertoire. <Client Name> read words, phrases, and sentences containing target consonant and vowel sounds in the initial, medial, and final positions of words. The following variations were noted (if the box is blank that indicates the target was produced).

Consonants									
Target	As in	Initial	Medial	Final	Target	As in	Initial	Medial	Final
t	to				d	do			
s	sew				z	zoo			
f	fun				v	van			
θ 'th'	thumb				ɹ 'r'	red			
l	light				n	no			
ʃ 'sh'	shoe				tʃ 'ch'	chew			
dʒ 'dg'	jump				ʒ 'zh'	Asia	■		
w	wild			■	h	hot			■
blends	clay		■	■					

Vowels						
Target	As in	Production	Target	As in	Production
i	eat		ʊ	hood	
ɪ	it		o	boat	
e	ate		a	hot	
ɛ	bed		ɔ	all	
æ	had		ɑɪ	bite	
ʌ	hut		ɑʊ	cow	
u	boot		ɔɪ	boy	

<No additional variations were noted in conversation / The following additional variations were noted in conversation:>

c. Intonation: Refers to the perception and production of rising and falling of intonation to indicate message meaning. <Client Name>'s results in perception and production of intonation are: Perception: <#> / 10 trials, < # > %   Production: <#> / 5 trials, < # > %

d. Syllable Stress: Refers to using prosodic features to stress the main syllable in a word with two or more syllables. <Client Name>'s results in syllable stress are: <#> / 10 trials, < # > %

e. Word Linking in Sentences: Refers to linking the end of a word to the beginning of another (e.g., consonant to subsequent same consonant; vowel to vowel; consonant to vowel). <Client Name>'s results in word linking are: <#> / 20 trials, < # > %

f. Auditory Discrimination: Refers to the ability to discriminate between sounds in words as being the same or similar. <Client Name>'s results in contrasting word and sentence pairs are:

Words: < # > / 15 trials, < # > %   Sentences: < # > / 5 trials, < # > %

g. Rate of Speech: Refers to the perceived rate of the speaker in a conversation. The average speaking rate is 120-150 words per minute. <Client Name> was judged to be a < # > on the following rating scale: 1) Slow   2) Natural rate   3) Fast

OBSERVATIONS

1. Volume: Refers to the speaker's loudness. <Client Name> was judged to be a < # > on the following rating scale: 1) Soft   2) Natural volume   3) Loud

2. Vocal Quality: Refers to the characteristics of vocal patterns. <Client Name>'s vocal quality was judged to be WNL <If not WNL, list other descriptors>

3. Vocal Resonance: Refers to the airflow as it passes through the pharyngeal, oral, and nasal cavities. <Client Name>'s vocal resonance was judged to be < oral / pharyngeal / nasal >

4. Grammar: Refers to the use of the structural rules of GenAm in spontaneous sentences and conversation. <No difficulties were noted in this area> OR <The following difficulties were noted:>

5. <u>Pragmatics:</u> Refers to the use of nonverbal language to relay the meaning of messages during interactions. <Client Name>'s use of pragmatics with a linguistically and culturally diverse conversation partner in the areas of eye contact, distance between speakers, topic maintenance, gestures, turn-taking, facial expressions, humor, and demeanor were judged to be WNL <If not, list areas of difficulty and describe:>

6. <u>Intelligibility:</u> <Client Name>'s overall intelligibility rating in conversation was judged to be < # > on the following rating scale:

☐ 1. Highly unintelligible

☐ 2. Intelligible in a known context

☐ 3. Distinct accent but intelligible

☐ 4. Intelligible with some trace of an accent

☐ 5. Nearly native

SUMMARY

<Choose one>:

<Client Name>'s intelligibility and naturalness were most impacted by: <list areas that should be addressed as noted above>. <Client Name> would benefit from accent modification to improve <his/her/their> production of General American English (GenAm) to increase overall intelligibility and naturalness in conversation. It is recommended that <Client Name> receive accent modification services <state frequency>.

OR

<Client Name> does not need to improve <his/her/their> production of General American English (GenAm). No services are recommended at this time.

RECOMMENDATIONS

The following is recommended for <Client Name>:

1. Accent modification <is/is not> recommended
2. See below for recommended goals
3. <State any other referrals or assessments recommended, if applicable>

Recommended Goals

Below is a list of short-term and long-term goals for <Client Name> based on the assessment results above.

<u>Long Term Goal 1</u>: <State long term goal > OR <Insert goals from Goal Bank>

Short Term Goal:
1.1 <State short term goal > OR <Insert goals from Goal Bank>
1.2 <State short term goal > OR <Insert goals from Goal Bank>
1.3 <State short term goal > OR <Insert goals from Goal Bank>

For further information, please feel free to contact <Your name> at <Phone Number> or email: <Email Address>

_____

<Name, Degree>

Suggested Goal Bank

Below is a goal bank with suggested goals you can copy and paste into the assessment report template. You should modify goals based on individual client needs.

Goals are organized into the following sections:

1. Long Term Goal

2. Segmentals

3. Suprasegmentals

4. Professional Speaking

Long Term Goal:

<Client Name> will improve the intelligibility and naturalness of spoken English in conversation in <academic / work / social> settings.

Short Term Goals:

1. Segmentals

<Client Name> will independently produce the target sound </   /> across 2 consecutive sessions in the following contexts:

a) Isolation or syllables in 4/5 trials

b) Initial, medial, final positions of words in 8/10 trials

c) All positions of words in phrases in 8/10 trials

d) All positions of words in sentences in 8/10 trials

e) All positions of words in short reading passages (2-4 sentences) in 4/5 trials

f) All positions of words in long reading passages (5+ sentences) with no more than 3 distinct variations

g) All positions of words in short spontaneous speech (1-3 sentences) in 4/5 trials

h) All positions of words in long spontaneous speech (3-5 minutes) with no more than 3 distinct variations

2. Suprasegmentals

Syllable Stress

<Client Name> will independently use prosodic features (loudness, vowel length, pitch change) to emphasize the stressed syllable of multisyllabic words across 2 consecutive sessions in the following contexts:

a) Words in 8/10 trials
b) Phrases in 8/10 trials
c) Sentences in 8/10 trials
d) Reading- Short Passages (2-4 sentences) in 4/5 trials
e) Reading- Long Passages (5+ sentences) with no more than 3 distinct variations
f) Spontaneous Speech- Short (1-3 sentences) in 4/5 trials
g) Spontaneous Speech- Long (3-5 minutes) with no more than 3 distinct variations

Intonation

<Client Name> will independently use rising or falling intonation to convey message meaning across 2 consecutive sessions in the following contexts:

a) Sentences in 8/10 trials
b) Reading- Short Passages (2-4 sentences) in 4/5 trials
c) Reading- Long Passages (5+ sentences) with no more than 3 distinct variations
d) Spontaneous Speech- Short (1-3 sentences) in 4/5 trials
e) Spontaneous Speech- Long (3-5 minutes) with no more than 3 distinct variations

Word Linking

<Client Name> will independently use co-articulation to link words together in longer utterances across 2 consecutive sessions in the following contexts:

Final consonant to subsequent same consonant (e.g., 'speaks Spanish')
Final consonant to subsequent vowel (e.g., 'Hold on')
Final vowel to subsequent vowel (e.g., 'I understand')

a) Sentences in 8/10 trials
b) Reading- Short Passages (2-4 sentences) in 4/5 trials
c) Reading- Long Passages (5+ sentences) with no more than 3 distinct variations
d) Spontaneous Speech- Short (1-3 sentences) in 4/5 trials
e) Spontaneous Speech- Long (3-5 minutes) with no more than 3 distinct variations

Pausing

<Client Name> will independently use appropriate pausing in thought groups across 2 consecutive sessions in the following contexts:

a) Sentences in 8/10 trials
b) Reading- Short Passages (2-4 sentences) in 4/5 trials
c) Reading- Long Passages (5+ sentences) with no more than 3 distinct variations
d) Spontaneous Speech- Short (1-3 sentences) in 4/5 trials
e) Spontaneous Speech- Long (3-5 minutes) with no more than 3 distinct variations

Key Words

<Client Name> will independently use prosodic features (pause, lengthening of last syllable, volume, intonation) to emphasize the key word in a thought group across 2 consecutive sessions in the following contexts:

a) Sentences in 8/10 trials
b) Reading- Short Passages (2-4 sentences) in 4/5 trials
c) Reading- Long Passages (5+ sentences) with no more than 3 distinct variations
d) Spontaneous Speech- Short (1-3 sentences) in 4/5 trials
e) Spontaneous Speech- Long (3-5 minutes) with no more than 3 distinct variations

Rate of Speech

<Client Name> will independently use a level 2 rate of speech in a 3-5 minute conversation on the following rating scale:

1) Slow   2) Natural rate   3) Fast

Volume

<Client Name> will independently maintain a level 2 volume in a 3-5 minute conversation on the following rating scale:

1) Soft   2) Natural volume   3) Loud

Resonance

<Client Name> will independently maintain an oral resonance in a 3-5 minute conversation

3. Professional Speaking

<Client Name> will independently utilize given professional speaking strategies in a 3-5 minute conversation

Accent Modification and Professional Speaking Assessment Report EXAMPLE			
Client Name:	Huan Lee	Preferred Name:	Huan
Pronouns:	He/Him/His	Date of Birth:	01/03/1988
Phone No:	202-111-3344	Email Address:	Client@gmail.com
Mailing Address:	123 St NW Washington, DC 20009		
Evaluator:	Kari Lim, M.S., CCC-SLP	Date of Report:	05/06/2020

REASON FOR REFERRAL

Huan Lee was self-referred for accent modification services. Huan reported that he has difficulty with pronouncing specific sounds: /n/, /m/, /ŋ/, grammar, understanding and being understood in social interactions, and using and understanding idioms and slang. He stated that these difficulties have negatively impacted his professional interactions, public speaking, career advancement, social interactions, and telephone conversations.

BACKGROUND INFORMATION

Huan is an adult male from China. His native language is Mandarin. Huan has lived in the U.S. for 7 years and 4 months. He has been speaking English for 17 years in total but only conversationally since he moved to the U.S. 7 years ago. Huan learned English in elementary school, and his instructors were not native English speakers. He is not fluent in any other languages.

Huan is in the last year of his Biomedical Engineering Doctoral program. He reported that he uses English 80% of the time during the week and 60% of the time on the weekends. Huan has received accent modification services since the Fall of 2019 and does not report a history of speech or language disorder in his native language.

ASSESSMENTS AND RESULTS

The following tools were administered in English on 05/06/2020:
1. Hearing Screening
2. Oral Mechanism Exam
3. Non-Standardized Assessment

The following areas of General American English (GenAm) were assessed:
a. Articulation
b. Intonation
c. Syllable Stress
d. Word Linking in Sentences
e. Auditory Discrimination
f. Rate of Speech

The assessment description and results are as follows:

1. Hearing Screening

Huan's hearing was screened in both the right and the left ears at 25 dB at 500 Hz, 1000 Hz, 2000 Hz, and 4000 Hz. Huan passed across all frequencies in both ears. He reported that he did not have concerns regarding his hearing.

2. Oral Mechanism Examination

An oral mechanism examination was administered to evaluate the structural and functional integrity of Huan's oral mechanism for speech production. Results are as follows:

Face: Overall appearance, symmetry, and tone appear to be within normal limits.

Jaw: Range of motion and strength appear to be within normal limits.

Lips: Range of motion, coordination, and strength appear to be within normal limits.

Teeth: Occlusion and structure appear to be within normal limits.

Tongue: Range of motion, coordination, and strength appear to be within normal limits.

Hard Palate: Structure and symmetry structure appear to be within normal limits.

Soft Palate: Structure, symmetry, and mobility appear to be within normal limits.

Diadochokinesis (DDK): Huan's ability to coordinate the production of syllables in rapid succession ("papapapa") and rapidly alternate speech movements ("pataka") are WNL.

3. Non-Standardized Assessment
*WNL = Within Normal Limits

a. <u>Articulation</u>: Refers to the production of sounds in the GenAm phonemic repertoire. Huan read words, phrases, and sentences containing target consonant and vowel sounds in the initial, medial, and final positions of words. The following variations were noted (if the box is blank that indicates the target was produced).

Consonants									
Target	As in	Initial	Medial	Final	Target	As in	Initial	Medial	Final
t	to				d	do		t	
s	sew				z	zoo			
f	fun				v	van			
θ 'th'	thumb			ð	ɹ 'r'	red			
l	light				n	no			ŋ
ʃ 'sh'	shoe				tʃ 'ch'	chew			
dʒ 'dg'	jump				ʒ 'zh'	Asia	■		dʒ
w	wild			■	h	hot			■
blends	clay		■	■					

Vowels					
Target	As in	Production	Target	As in	Production
i	eat	e, ɪ	ʊ	hood	u
ɪ	it	i	o	boat	
e	ate		a	hot	
ɛ	bed	i	ɔ	all	
æ	had		ɑɪ	bite	
ʌ	hut		ɑʊ	cow	ɔ
u	boot		ɔɪ	boy	

Huan was noted to delete final consonants of multisyllabic words in conversation.

c. <u>Intonation</u>: Refers to the perception and production of rising and falling of intonation to indicate message meaning. Huan's results in perception and production of intonation are: Perception: 8/10 trials, 80%   Production: 4/5 trials, 80%

d. <u>Syllable Stress</u>: Refers to using prosodic features to stress the main syllable in a word with two or more syllables. Huan's results in syllable stress are: 8/10 trials, 80%

e. <u>Word Linking in Sentences:</u> Refers to linking the end of a word to the beginning of another (consonant to subsequent same consonant; vowel to vowel; consonant to vowel). Huan's results in word linking are: 17/20 trials, 85%

f. <u>Auditory Discrimination:</u> Refers to the ability to discriminate between sounds in words as being the same or similar. Huan's results in contrasting word and sentence pairs are: Words: 13/15 trials, 87%   Sentences: 4/5 trials, 80%

g. <u>Rate of Speech:</u> Refers to the perceived rate of the speaker in a conversation. The average speaking rate is 120-150 words per minute. Huan was judged to be a 2 on the following rating scale: 1) Slow   2) Natural rate   3) Fast

OBSERVATIONS

1. <u>Volume:</u> Refers to the speaker's loudness. Huan was judged to be a 3 on the following rating scale: 1) Soft   2) Natural volume   3) Loud

2. <u>Vocal Quality:</u> Refers to the characteristics of vocal patterns. Huan's vocal quality was judged to be WNL.

3. <u>Vocal Resonance:</u> Refers to the airflow as it passes through the pharyngeal, oral, and nasal cavities. Huan's vocal resonance was judged to be oral.

4. <u>Grammar:</u> Refers to the use of the structural rules of GenAm in spontaneous sentences and conversation. No difficulties were noted in this area.

5. <u>Pragmatics:</u> Refers to the use of nonverbal language to relay the meaning of messages during interactions. Huan's use of pragmatics with a linguistically and culturally diverse conversation partner in the areas of eye contact, distance between speakers, topic maintenance, gestures, turn-taking, facial expressions, humor, and demeanor were judged to be WNL.

6. <u>Intelligibility:</u> Huan's overall intelligibility rating in conversation was judged to be 3 on the following rating scale:
☐ 1. Highly unintelligible
☐ 2. Intelligible in a known context
☒ 3. Distinct accent but intelligible
☐ 4. Intelligible with some trace of an accent
☐ 5. Nearly native

SUMMARY

Huan's intelligibility was most impacted by final consonant deletions, syllable stress, and consonants and vowel variations. Huan would benefit from accent modification to improve his production of General American English (GenAm) to increase overall intelligibility in conversation. It is recommended that Huan receive accent modification services 1x/week for 50-minute sessions.

RECOMMENDATIONS

The following is recommended for Huan Lee.
1. Accent modification is recommended 1x/week for 50 minutes
2. See below for recommended goals

Recommended Goals
Below is a list of short-term and long-term goals for Huan Lee based on the assessment results above.

Long Term Goal 1: Huan will improve the intelligibility and naturalness of spoken English in conversation in academic and social settings.

Short Term Goal:
1.1 Huan will independently produce the target sound /θ/ across 2 consecutive sessions in the following contexts:
 a) Isolation or syllables in 4/5 trials
 b) Initial, medial, final positions of words in 8/10 trials
 c) All positions of words in phrases in 8/10 trials
 d) All positions of words in sentences in 8/10 trials
 e) All positions of words in short reading passages (2-4 sentences) in 4/5 trials
 f) All positions of words in long reading passages (5+ sentences) with no more than 3 distinct variations
 g) All positions of words in short spontaneous speech (1-3 sentences) in 4/5 trials
 h) All positions of words in long spontaneous speech (3-5 minutes) with no more than 3 distinct variations

1.2 Huan will independently produce the target sound /i/ across 2 consecutive sessions in the following contexts:

a) Initial, medial, final positions of words in 8/10 trials
b) All positions of words in phrases in 8/10 trials
c) All positions of words in sentences in 8/10 trials
d) All positions of words in short reading passages (2-4 sentences) in 4/5 trials
e) All positions of words in long reading passages (5+ sentences) with no more than 3 distinct variations
f) All positions of words in short spontaneous speech (1-3 sentences) in 4/5 trials
g) All positions of words in long spontaneous speech (3-5 minutes) with no more than 3 distinct variations

1.3 Huan will independently maintain a level 2 volume in a 3-5 minute conversation on the following rating scale:
1) Soft   2) Natural volume   3) Loud

1.4 Huan will independently use appropriate pausing in thought groups across 2 consecutive sessions in the following contexts:

a) Sentences in 8/10 trials
b) Reading- Short Passages (2-4 sentences) in 4/5 trials
c) Reading- Long Passages (5+ sentences) with no more than 3 distinct variations
d) Spontaneous Speech- Short (1-3 sentences) in 4/5 trials
e) Spontaneous Speech- Long (3-5 minutes) with no more than 3 distinct variations

1.5 Huan will independently use prosodic features (pause, lengthening of last syllable, volume, intonation) to emphasize the key word in a thought group across 2 consecutive sessions in the following contexts:

a) Sentences in 8/10 trials
b) Reading- Short Passages (2-4 sentences) in 4/5 trials
c) Reading- Long Passages (5+ sentences) with no more than 3 distinct variations
d) Spontaneous Speech- Short (1-3 sentences) in 4/5 trials
e) Spontaneous Speech- Long (3-5 minutes) with no more than 3 distinct variations

1.6 Huan will independently utilize given professional speaking strategies in a 3–5-minute conversation

For further information, please feel free to contact Kari Lim at 202-111-2222 or email: Kari@globalspeechtherapy.com.

Kari Lim, M.S., CCC-SLP

Kari Lim, M.S., CCC-SLP

Screener Areas

This screener is a great alternative for clients who do not want or need a full assessment. This English pronunciation screener takes approximately 10-15 minutes to administer and rate the intelligibility and naturalness of speakers.

Instructor Packet: Sections for instructors to complete during the screener

Section A. *Stimulus Words:* Rates the client's productions of consonants and vowels in GenAm in words

Section B. *Reading Passage:* Rates the client's sound production in structured, connected speech

Section C. *Conversational Sample* (not to be transcribed)*:* An observational tool that rates the client's sound production and vocal qualities in spontaneous, connected speech

Client Stimuli: Stimuli for the client to read during the screener

Instructor Packet

Client Information (have client fill in this page)

Name: _____

Preferred name: _____ Preferred pronouns: _____

Date: _____ Phone: _____(home / work / cell)

Native Language/s: _____

Native Country: _____

Employer or Academic Program: _____

Email Address: _____

How would you rate <u>your</u> pronunciation of English (check one)?
☐ 1. Highly unintelligible
☐ 2. Intelligible in a known context
☐ 3. Distinct accent but intelligible
☐ 4. Intelligible with some trace of an accent
☐ 5. Nearly native

A. <u>Stimulus Words</u>

Instruction: Have the client read the stimulus words from the *Client Stimuli*. Note any consonant and vowel variations heard.

Note – Corresponds to section A of the Client Stimuli. Your best guide is to describe those features that other native lay speakers would notice. If necessary, ask the client to speak slower or to repeat the word.

Say to the client: "Please read each word aloud once. Speak in your natural voice."

Word	Target 1	Target 2	Target 3
1. **Sign**	/s/	/ɑɪ/	/n/
2. **Off**	/a/	/f/	----
3. **Thin**	/θ/	/ɪ/	/n/
4. **Ring**	/ɹ/	/i/	/ŋ/
5. **Yell**	/j/	/ɛ/	/l/
6. **Choose**	/tʃ/	/u/	/z/
7. **Asia**	/e/	/ʒ/	/ʌ/
8. **Wise**	/w/	/ɑɪ/	/z/
9. **Help**	/h/	/ɛ/	/lp/
10. **Jump**	/dʒ/	/ʌ/	/mp/
11. **Void**	/v/	/ɔɪ/	/d/
12. **Face**	/f/	/e/	/s/
13. **Match**	/m/	/æ/	/tʃ/
14. **Shop**	/ʃ/	/a/	/p/
15. **Proud**	/pr/	/aʊ/	/d/
16. **Sleeve**	/sl/	/i/	/v/
17. **Leap**	/l/	/i/	/p/
18. **Caught**	/k/	/ɔ/	/t/
19. **Good**	/g/	/ʊ/	/d/
20. **Toast**	/t/	/o/	/st/

B. Reading Passage

Instruction: Have the client read the reading passage from the *Client Stimuli*. Note any consonant and vowel variations heard in the space below.

Note – Corresponds to section B of the Client Stimuli. Your best guide is to describe those features that other native lay speakers would notice. If necessary, ask the client to speak slower or to repeat the word.

Say to the client: "Read the following paragraph out loud. Speak in your natural voice."

The Grandfather Passage
By Charles Van Riper

You wished to know all about my grandfather. Well, he is nearly ninety-three years old. He dresses himself in an ancient black frock coat, usually minus several buttons; yet he still thinks as swiftly as ever. A long, flowing beard clings to his chin, giving those who observe him a pronounced feeling of the utmost respect. When he speaks his voice is just a bit cracked and quivers a trifle. Twice each day he plays skillfully and with zest upon our small organ. Except in the winter when the ooze or snow or ice prevents, he slowly takes a short walk in the open air each day. We have often urged him to walk more and smoke less, but he always answers, "Banana Oil!" Grandfather likes to be modern in his language.

Instructor Notes:

C. Conversation Speech Sample

Instruction: Have the client speak for 2 minutes on a chosen topic. Note any variations or patterns that impact overall intelligibility and naturalness in conversation. Say to the client: "Now I want you to talk for about 2 minutes. I will time you. You can talk about your field of study or job, hobbies or interests, or any other topic. Speak in your natural voice." Other prompts: favorite meals, describe a native country, favorite holidays

Note – There are no client stimuli for this section. You do not need to focus on narrow transcription. Your best guide is to describe those features that other native lay speakers would notice.

Observation Ratings

Rate of Speech: ☐ Slow ☐ Natural Rate ☐ Fast

Volume: ☐ Soft ☐ Natural Volume ☐ Loud

Intonation & Stress: ☐ Monotone ☐ Appropriate ☐ Too Much

Resonance: ☐ Nasal ☐ Oral ☐ Pharyngeal

Vocal Quality: ☐ WNL* ☐ Raspy ☐ Breathy ☐ Other:

Grammar: ☐ WNL* ☐ Difficulties Noted:
WNL: Within Normal Limits

Instructor Notes:

Overall intelligibility was judged to be:
☐ 1. Highly unintelligible
☐ 2. Intelligible in a known context
☐ 3. Distinct accent but intelligible
☐ 4. Intelligible with some trace of an accent
☐ 5. Nearly native

Client Stimuli

Client instructions: You have stimuli for only the sections that you need. Wait for the Instructor to give you instructions for each subtest.

A. Stimulus Words

1. Sign

2. Off

3. Thin

4. Ring

5. Yell

6. Choose

7. Asia

8. Wise

9. Help

10. Jump

11. Void

12. Face

13. Match

14. Shop

15. Proud

16. Sleeve

17. Leap

18. Caught

19. Good

20. Toast

B. <u>Reading Passage</u>

<u>The Grandfather Passage</u>
By Charles Van Riper

You wished to know all about my grandfather. Well, he is nearly ninety-three years old. He dresses himself in an ancient black frock coat, usually minus several buttons; yet he still thinks as swiftly as ever. A long, flowing beard clings to his chin, giving those who observe him a pronounced feeling of the utmost respect. When he speaks his voice is just a bit cracked and quivers a trifle. Twice each day he plays skillfully and with zest upon our small organ. Except in the winter when the ooze or snow or ice prevents, he slowly takes a short walk in the open air each day. We have often urged him to walk more and smoke less, but he always answers, "Banana Oil!" Grandfather likes to be modern in his language.

References

Patel, R., Connaghan, K., Franco, D., Edsall, E., Forgit, D., Olsen, L., Ramage, L., Tyler, E., & Russell, S. (2013). "The caterpillar": a novel reading passage for assessment of motor speech disorders. American Journal of Speech-Language Pathology, 22(1), 1–9. https://doi.org/10.1044/1058-0360(2012/11-01

Section 4

Segmentals

<u>Overview</u>

Simply put, segmentals refer to speech sounds - both consonants and vowels. These sounds are produced using our 'articulators.' These include the:

- Lips
- Teeth- upper and lower
- Tongue
- Mandible- lower jaw
- Alveolar Ridge- gum ridge behind top teeth
- Hard and Soft Palate- roof of mouth
- Larynx- voice box which includes epiglottis, vocal folds, and trachea
- Nose
- Pharynx- throat

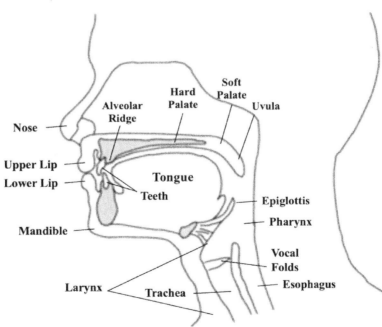

Figure 4-1. Articulators

Consonants

In General American English (GenAm), there are 24 consonant sounds. Consonants are categorized by place, manner, and voicing.

1. **Place**: refers to the articulators that work together to produce a sound. For example, /p, b/ are considered bilabials, meaning they are produced using your top and bottom lip, and /f, v/ are considered labiodental, meaning they are produced using your bottom lip and top teeth.

2. **Manner**: refers to how the air flows through the articulators. For example, /p, b/ are considered 'stops,' meaning that airflow is completely blocked by the lips, and /f, v/ are considered 'fricatives,' meaning that the lower lip and upper teeth partially block airflow.

3. **Voicing:** refers to the activity of the vocal folds in the voice box. When the vocal folds are apart and not vibrating, the sound is voiceless (p, f). When the vocal folds are together and vibrating, the sound is voiced (b, v).

Figure 4-2 below is an example of where sounds are produced in the mouth.

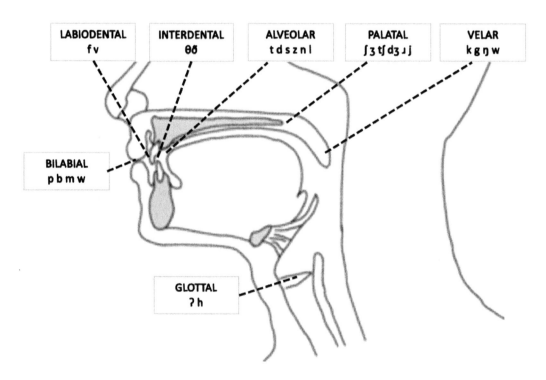

Figure 4-2. Place, Manner, and Voicing

A quick note about IPA (International Phonetic Alphabet): Not all professional backgrounds learn IPA, or use it consistently, and that is ok! IPA isn't an easy shortcut. It takes critical thinking to describe what you hear. It should be an interactive dialogue with others because we all hear things differently the first, second, third time, and beyond when listening to a speech sample over and over. So, while most of the sounds below are transcribed with IPA, it's perfectly acceptable to develop your own system of documenting what you hear. Your notes should answer this question "How do I want to communicate this to myself?" As one is exposed to more sounds/accents/dialects, there is increased understanding of all the IPA symbols and diacritics.

Table 4-1. Place Manner and Voicing Chart

Manner	Voicing	Bilabial — Formed by closure of lips	Labiodental — Formed with lips and teeth	Interdental — Formed with tongue between teeth	Alveolar — Formed with tongue tip touching alveolar ridge	Palatal — Formed with body of tongue touching palate	Velar — Formed with back of tongue touching roof of mouth	Glottal — Formed by obstructing airflow in vocal tract
Stop — Airflow is blocked	Voiceless	p (as in 'pen')			t (as in 'two')		k (as in 'can')	ʔ (as in 'uh-oh')
Stop — Airflow is blocked	Voiced	b (as in 'bat')			d (as in 'dog')		g (as in 'go')	
Fricative — Airflow is partially blocked	Voiceless		f (as in 'fish')	θ (as in 'think')	s (as in 'sit')	ʃ 'sh' (as in 'shoe')		h (as in 'he')
Fricative — Airflow is partially blocked	Voiced		v (as in 'van')	ð (as in 'the')	z (as in 'zoo')	ʒ 'zh' (as in 'beige')		
Affricate — Begins as stop and ends with fricative	Voiceless					tʃ 'ch' (as in 'chew')		
Affricate — Begins as stop and ends with fricative	voiced					dʒ 'dg' (as in 'jump')		
Nasal — Airflow passes through nose	Voiced	m (as in 'me')			n (as in 'no')		ŋ 'ng' (as in 'ring')	
Liquid — Tongue forms partial closure in mouth	Voiced				l (as in 'lot')			
Liquid — Tongue forms partial closure in mouth	Voiced					r (as in 'red')		
Glide — Like vowel but functions as consonant	Voiced	w (as in 'we')				j 'y' (as in 'yes')	w (as in 'we')	

Table 4-1. Place, Manner, and Voicing Chart

Common Consonant Patterns

Consonants can occur in 3 positions of words.

1. **Initial**: beginning of words, like /f/ in 'fish'
2. **Medial:** middle of words, like /f/ in 'muffin'
3. **Final:** end of words, like /f/ in 'puff'

Languages have different rules for what sounds can occur in each word position. For example, in GenAm, there is no 'ng' in the initial part of words, but it is in the medial and final positions (e.g., singer, ring).

Languages also differ by their phonological repertoires, or the inventory of speech sounds. For example, Spanish doesn't have the /z/ sound as in 'zoo,' and Mandarin does not have blends like the /sl/ in 'slide.' English consonants that are considered uncommon in other languages are

Consonants	Typical Substitution
/ð, θ/ voiced and voiceless 'th' as in 'the' and 'think'	t, d, f
/z/ as in 'zoo'	s
/dʒ/ 'dg' as in 'jump'	'zh' or 'y'
/ɹ/ American 'r' as in 'red'	flapped or trilled r

Table 4-2. Uncommon English Consonants

Not all substitutions will impact intelligibility greatly, such as r/ɹ, s/z, ʃ/ʒ, but these can impact a speaker's naturalness. For sounds that General American English and other languages have in common, they may be pronounced slightly differently. For example, the /t/ in GenAm is produced just behind the alveolar ridge (gum ridge behind top teeth), but in Hindi, the /t/ is produced farther back. Also, native English speakers tend to speak with a bit more 'punch' at the beginning of words, but the ending of words do not have the same 'punch.' However, native English speakers use less muscular tension, or force, on consonants and vowels compared to other languages.

While you will usually address subtle differences in sound production, such as more/less aspiration or a slight change in tongue position, here are common patterns noted in accent modification.

Pattern	Description	Example
Devoicing of sounds	Substituting a voiceless sound for a voiced sound	'to' for 'do'
Voicing of sounds	Substituting a voiced sound for a voiceless sound	'do' for 'to'
Deletion of final consonants (DFC)	Deleting sounds at the end of words	'baugh' for 'ball'
Epenthesis	Adding a schwa or 'uh' in words in initial, medial, or final positions as well as in blends	'suhlide' for 'slide'
Substitutions	Substituting one sound for another	'night' for 'light'
Distortions or approximations	Producing a variation of the target sound	Producing /s/ with a frontal distortion, or lisp

Table 4-3. Common Patterns

'R' and 'L'

A quick note about the two most difficult sounds to produce in English, the 'R' and 'L':

R

/ɹ/ can be the most difficult sound to produce for both native and non-native speakers because there are no oral landmarks. In all other consonants in English, the articulators make contact with each other. For /ɹ/, the tongue is just hanging out in the oral cavity. Some languages don't have this sound, or it is produced as flapped, with the tongue tip behind the alveolar ridge like a /d/ sound or trilled, like the rolled 'R' in Spanish.

There are two ways to produce the GenAm /ɹ/- bunched vs. retroflex. These are just how they sound. For the bunched /ɹ/, the tongue is pulled back, or bunched up, with the sides close to the top teeth. Some people use the image of a mountain. For the retroflex /ɹ/, the tongue tip is curled up and backward like a 'C.'

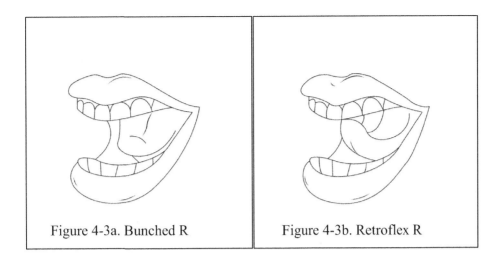

| Figure 4-3a. Bunched R | Figure 4-3b. Retroflex R |

Lastly, vocalic /ɹ/, which refers to any /ɹ/ that follows a vowel, like -er and -air, takes on vocalic properties depending on what vowel comes before it. Typically -er, as in 'earth,' is the most difficult, especially the blend –erl as in 'girl, world.' So, this means there are many types of /ɹ/ productions to learn.

L

While /l/ does have oral landmarks, it can be difficult to hear in words, especially in medial and final positions. Brains fill in the blanks with what they think they heard, which is why errors typically occur more in the medial and final position of words than initial position. This sound can be colored by vowels as well, just like vocalic /ɹ/. Additionally, some languages interchange r/l without changing the meaning of the word.

For words containing /ɹ/ and /l/ blends, such as "slide" or "broom," it's best to address these sounds individually in the initial, medial, and final position of words before having clients practice them in blends.

Discuss

Read the following prompts to the client so they can think about their articulators, airflow, and voicing.
1. Produce the following sounds and tell me what articulators you are using: p, b, v, f, k, g, s, z
2. Produce the following sounds and tell me which ones you can hold out (have continuous airflow): p, b, v, f, k, g, s, z
3. Produce the following sounds and tell me which ones are voiced (have vocal fold vibration): p, b, v, f, k, g, s, z

Choosing Consonant Targets

Some of your clients will only have a few consonants to address, but others will have many. To prioritize goals, consider the following.

1. **Contrastive analysis:** target sounds that do not occur in the client's L1
   Example: /z/ for a Spanish speaker
   English consonants that are considered uncommon in other languages: /ð, θ, z, ʒ, ɹ/
2. **Occurrence rate**: target sounds that occur most frequently in English
   Example: /s/ is more common than /ʒ/
3. **Functional load:** target sounds in which variations produce real words vs. non-words
   Example: Rich/Reach as in "Rich for it" vs. "Reach for it"
   Variations that produce real words are more difficult for the listener to use context clues to decipher meaning
4. **Impact on intelligibility:** target sounds that most impact intelligibility
   Example: r/ɹ, s/z, ʃ/ʒ

Remember that languages have different rules for sound production, so even if a sound occurs in the client's native language, the production may be different. You may find yourself working on subtle differences, such as more/less aspiration or a slight change in tongue placement. For example, Hindi speakers may use a retroflex /t/.

Articulation Hierarchy

A systematic way to address segmentals is to use the traditional articulation hierarchy. In this hierarchy, sounds are addressed in the following order:
1. Isolation and/or syllables
2. Initial, medial, final positions of words
3. All positions of words in phrases
4. All positions of words in sentences
5. All positions of words in short reading passages (2-4 sentences)
6. All positions of words in long reading passages (5+ sentences)
7. All positions of words in short spontaneous speech (1-3 sentences)
8. All positions of words in long spontaneous speech (3-5 minutes)

Initially, sounds should be introduced individually, in one-word position (initial, medial, or final) and in 1 syllable words. As the client progresses, the instructor can quickly increase word length to 2-3 syllables, introduce other word positions, and target more than one sound in each trial.

As mentioned earlier, accent modification is more than just sounds. One needs to work on how sounds are produced in words as well as phrases and sentences because sounds are influenced by the other sounds that come before and after them. This is called coarticulation. For example, /t/ in the word 'that' changes in the following ways:
- In the single word 'that' the /t/ is a hard, aspirated sound
- In the phrase 'that dog' the /t/ becomes dropped for the /d/ sound
- In the phrase 'that one' the /t/ becomes a glottal stop

Consonant Practice Stimuli

There are lots of resources online for consonant stimuli. Two recommended free websites for consonant word lists that are adult-friendly (no pictures) are:
a. Tools for Clear Speech: https://tfcs.baruch.cuny.edu/consonants-vowels/
b. Home Speech Home Word Lists: https://www.home-speech-home.com/speech-therapy-word-lists.html

Remember the acronym **M.O.T.O.R**. Below is a suggestion for targeting /s/ in the initial position of words using the formats.

			Table 4-4. Formats for Practice	
	Format	**Instructor Utterance**		**Client Utterance**
M	**Model**	"Say Sam"		"Sam"
O	**Opposites**	"Say Sam, tham"		"Sam, tham"
T	**Tell apart**	"Which one is the target: Sam or tham"		"First one"
O	**Over-Correction**	"Say Ssssam"		"Ssssam"
R	**Resay**	N/A		"Sam"

Table 4-5 below explains the manner, place, and voicing for all consonants in GenAm as well as a description of how to produce the sound and common variations produced by accent modification clients.

Table 4-5. Consonant Elicitation Techniques

Sound	Place	Manner	Voicing	Elicitation Technique	Common Variations
/p/	Bilabial	Stop	No	Bring your lips together, open your lips quickly while blowing air forward, and say 'puh'	Voicing /b/, unaspirated
/b/	Bilabial	Stop	Yes	/b/ is like /p/ but voiced and less breathy. Bring your lips together, open your lips quickly, turn your voice on, and say 'buh'	Devoicing /p/, aspirated
/t/	Alveolar	Stop	No	Slightly open your mouth, touch your tongue blade to the gums behind your top teeth and quickly pull the tongue back while blowing air forward, and say 'tuh'	Voicing /d/, laminal-alveolar, flap, dental, unaspirated
/d/	Alveolar	Stop	Yes	/d/ is like /t/ but voiced and less breathy. Slightly open your mouth, touch your tongue blade to the gums behind your top teeth and quickly pull the tongue back, and say 'duh'	Devoicing /t/, laminal-alveolar, flap, dental, unaspirated
/k/	Velar	Stop	No	Slightly open your mouth, raise the base of your tongue to the back of your mouth and quickly pull the tongue down while blowing air forward, and say 'kuh'	Voicing /g/, guttural, unaspirated
/g/	Velar	Stop	Yes	/g/ is like /k/ but voiced. Slightly open your mouth, raise the base of your tongue to the back of your mouth and quickly pull the tongue down, turn your voice on, and say 'guh'	Devoicing /k/, guttural, aspirated
/f/	Labio-dental	Fricative	No	Bite your bottom lip with your top teeth, blow air forward, and say 'fff'	Voicing /v/, stop /t/, unaspirated

Sound	Place	Manner	Voicing	Elicitation Technique	Common Variations
/v/	Labio-dental	Fricative	Yes	/v/ is like /f/ but voiced. Bite your bottom lip with your top teeth, turn your voice on, and say 'vvv'	Devoicing /f/, stop /b/, aspirated
/θ/ voiceless 'th'	Inter-dental	Fricative	No	Slightly lower your jaw, stick your tongue tip between your teeth, blow air forward, and say 'th'	Voicing /ð/, laminal-alveolar /s/, stop /t/, unaspirated
/ð/ voiced 'th'	Inter-dental	Fricative	Yes	/ð/ is like /θ/ but voiced. Slightly lower your jaw, stick your tongue tip between your teeth, turn your voice on, and say 'th'	Devoicing /θ/, laminal-alveolar /z/, stop /d/, aspirated
/s/	Alveolar	Fricative	No	Close your mouth so your top and bottom teeth are barely touching, slightly open your lips, put your tongue blade slightly behind your top teeth, blow air forward, and say 'sss'	Voicing /z/, stop /t/, frontal or lateral distortion
/z/	Alveolar	Fricative	Yes	/z/ is like /s/ but voiced. Close your mouth so your top and bottom teeth are barely touching, slightly open your lips, put your tongue blade slightly behind your top teeth, turn your voice on, and say 'zzz'	Devoicing /s/, stop /d/, frontal or lateral distortion
/ʃ/ 'sh'	Palatal	Fricative	No	Slightly open your mouth, raise your tongue so sides of the tongue are touching the upper back teeth, blow air forward, and say 'shhh' Other: If the client can produce /s/, have them say 'sss' and pull their tongue backward to produce 'shhh'	Voicing /ʒ/, laminal-alveolar /s/, affrication /tʃ/, lateral distortion

Sound	Place	Manner	Voicing	Elicitation Technique	Common Variations
/ʒ/ 'zh'	Palatal	Fricative	Yes	/ʒ/ is like /ʃ/ but voiced. Slightly open your mouth, raise your tongue so sides of the tongue are touching the upper back teeth, turn your voice on, and say 'zhhh' Other: If the client can say /z/, have them say 'zzz' and pull their tongue backward to produce 'zhhh'	Devoicing /ʃ/, laminal-alveolar /z/, affrication /dʒ/, lateral distortion
/h/	Glottal	Fricative	No	Slightly open your mouth, blow air forward, and say 'hhh'	Voicing, guttural
/tʃ/ 'ch'	Palatal	Affricate	No	Close your mouth so your teeth are barely touching, slightly open your lips and round them, raise your tongue so sides of the tongue are touching the upper back teeth and quickly pull the tongue back, and say 'chuh'	Voicing /dʒ/, stop /t/, lateral distortion, deaffrication /ʃ/
/dʒ/ 'dg'	Palatal	Affricate	Yes	/dʒ/ is like /tʃ/ but voiced. Close your mouth so your teeth are barely touching, slightly open your lips and round them, raise your tongue so sides of the tongue are touching the upper back teeth and quickly pull the tongue back, turn your voice on, and say 'juh'	Devoicing /tʃ/, stop /d/, lateral distortion, deaffrication /ʒ/
/m/	Bilabial	Nasal	Yes	Close your lips, turn your voice on, blow air up and through your nose, and say 'mmm'	Aspirated, stopping
/n/	Alveolar	Nasal	Yes	Slightly open your mouth, touch your tongue blade to the gums behind your top teeth, blow air up and through your nose, turn your voice on, and say 'nnn'	Stopping, back-velar /ŋ/, dental, liquid /l/

Sound	Place	Manner	Voicing	Elicitation Technique	Common Variations
/ŋ/ 'ng'	Velar	Nasal	Yes	Slightly open your mouth, raise the base of your tongue to the back of your mouth, push air up and through your nose, turn your voice on, and say 'ng'	Stopping, denasalization /n/
/j/ 'y'	Palatal	Glide	Yes	Slightly open your mouth, keep your tongue flat and forward towards your teeth, then pull back and open your mouth, turn your voice on, and say 'yuh'	Unrounding, jaw height
/w/	Velar	Glide	Yes	Slightly open your mouth, round your lips and pull them back, turn your voice on, and say 'wuh'	Frication /hw/ or /v/
/ɹ/	Palatal	Liquid	Yes	**Retroflex:** Slightly open your mouth, pull your tongue tip back and point it towards the roof of your mouth, add slight tension to your tongue (squeeze), turn your voice on, and say 'ruh' (or 'err') **Bunched:** Point the tip of your tongue towards the roof of your mouth so the sides are touching your back teeth, add slight tension to your tongue (squeeze), lift the body of your tongue down behind your bottom teeth, turn your voice on, and say 'ruh' (or 'err')	Gliding /w/, trill, flap, nonrhotacization (vowel)
/l/	Alveolar	Liquid	Yes	Slightly open your mouth, touch your tongue blade to the gums behind your top teeth, turn your voice on, and say 'lll'	Gliding /w/ or /j/, rhotacization /ɹ/, rounding

Vowels

In General American English, there are about 3 times the number of vowels compared to other languages. Because of this, regional dialects in the U.S. are easily distinguished by vowel production. For example, with the two words 'pen' and 'pin,' in the northern U.S., they are pronounced differently, but in the southern U.S., they are pronounced the same. This feature has its own name, the *pen/pin merger.*

A good reference for vowels is the Standard Lexical Sets created by John C. Wells, in which he references two accents, General American English (GenAm) and Received Pronunciation (RP, a British dialect). Below is a chart for GenAm with the keyword, IPA symbol, and example words.

Keyword	IPA Symbol	Example Words
Face	e	Name, Pay, Hey
Dress	ɛ	Egg, Neck, Rest
Fleece	i	Eat, Leap, Me
Goat	o	Road, Soak, Phone
Kit	ɪ	It, Rip, Did
Trap	æ	Flat, Glad, Nap
Strut	ʌ	Up, Just, Shut
Lot	a	Got, Lock, Swap
Thought	ɔ	Aw, Gone, All
Foot	ʊ	Bush, Put, Took
Goose	u	Mood, Juice, Move
Price	aɪ	Hi, Bye, My
Choice	ɔɪ	Toy, Boy, Joy
Mouth	aʊ	Ow, Cow, Loud

Table 4-6. Lexical Sets. Adapted from: Lexical Set (2021).

Distinctive features

All vowels are voiced, while about only half of English consonants are, and are most influenced by 3 distinctive features. The distinctive features are:

1. Jaw height
2. Tongue placement
3. Lip roundedness

Because of the number of vowels in GenAm, that means that there is more movement in the oral cavity to produce vowels, making vowels difficult for non-native speakers. The changes in jaw height, tongue position, and lip roundedness are very slight. More attention is usually given to vowels than consonants in accent modification sessions.

Vowel Chart

Below you will find a vowel chart. Since most people aren't familiar with the International Phonetic Alphabet (IPA), orthographic words are matched with the symbol. However, you still need a basic understanding of how the words are produced with a native GenAm accent.

The 3 distinctive vowel features can be seen in the vowel chart.

1. **Jaw Height:** The vertical axis refers to the jaw height. Think of the jaw as having 3 planes or levels of opening
   a. Slightly open (high)
   b. Moderately open (mid)
   c. Widely open (low)
2. **Tongue Placement:** The horizontal axis refers to tongue placement. There are 3 placements
   a. Front of mouth
   b. Central (middle of mouth)
   c. Back of mouth
3. **Lip Roundedness:** The horizontal axis also refers to lip roundedness. Lips are:
   a. Rounded
   b. Unrounded
   There is one exception here. For the vowel /i/ ('e' as in green), the lips are pulled back, or retracted.

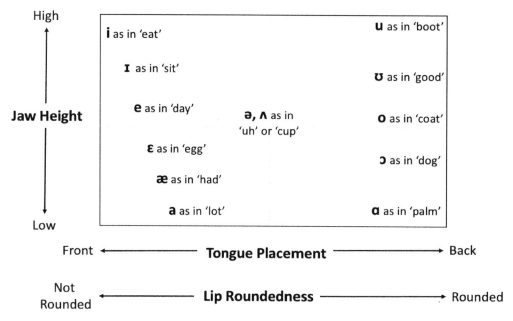

Figure 4-4. Vowel Chart

Because tongue movement is so slight, the easiest way to think about vowels is to think about jaw height. If the client has difficulty with vowel production, have them open and close the mouth until they are able to produce the target sound. Changing jaw height automatically changes tongue position. If the mouth is widely open, the tongue has more room to move. If the mouth is only slightly open, there is limited room for tongue movement. Note: it's difficult to produce most vowels in isolation, so starting with syllables or words is best.

Discuss

1. Have the client produce a sustained 'ah' sound and open and close their jaw. Discuss how the vowel sound changes with jaw height.

2. Have the client produce a sustained 'ah' sound and protrude and retract their lips. Discuss how the vowel sound changes with lip roundedness.

Diphthongs

A diphthong is formed by the blend of two vowels in a single syllable, in which the sound begins as one vowel and moves toward another. For example:
1. 'ow' as in 'cow'
2. 'I' as in 'hi'
3. 'oy' as in 'toy'

Below is a vowel chart showing how vowels in GenAm are blended to form a diphthong.

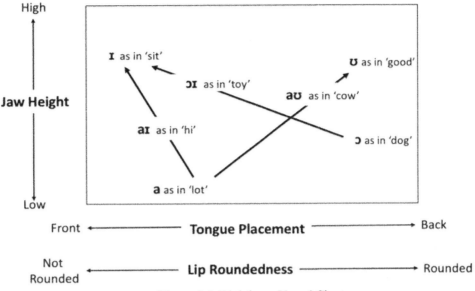

Figure 4-5. Diphthong Vowel Chart

Vowel Length

Some vowels in GenAm are naturally elongated, and others are short. Vowel length can impact the rate of speech; if you produce short vowels, you will speak at a faster rate and vice versa.

One-syllable words that end in a voiced consonant have a longer vowel than words that end in an unvoiced sound. For example:
1. Lab vs. lap
2. Cob vs. cop
3. Mob vs. mop

Words that are 2 or more syllables have shorter vowel sounds. The shorter vowels in 2+ syllable words, which are unstressed, are typically replaced with a *schwa*, or 'uh' sound. For example,

1. Can vs. Canada (Can-uh-duh)
2. Ban vs. banana (buh-na-nuh)
3. Cart vs. carton (car-tuhn)

Discuss

Read the words to the client and ask them to tell you which ones are longer (**bolded** words).

Word 1	Word 2
Beet	**Bead**
Bet	**Bed**
Bud	But
Lock	**Log**
Comb	Cope
Leaf	**Leave**
Badge	Batch
Mace	**Maze**
Seize	Cease
Teeth	**Teethe**

Table 4-7. Vowel Length Practice

Now have the client use the previous words in the following sentences and try to hold out the longer vowel.

1. The bead looks like a beet.
2. I bet you can find a bed at the store.
3. The flower bud is pretty but not blooming.
4. The lock on the log is to keep it in place.
5. He will have to cope with just a comb.
6. Leave the leaf on the ground.
7. Show your badge for a batch of cookies.
8. Don't bring mace on the maze.
9. They will seize and then cease.
10. Babies who teethe are growing teeth.

Choosing Vowel Targets

Similar to consonants, when choosing vowels to target, consider:
1. What sounds do not occur in the client's L1
2. How frequently the sound occurs in English
3. If variations produce real words vs. non-words
4. Impact on intelligibility

Remember the articulation hierarchy (isolation/syllables, words, phrases, sentences, reading passages aloud, spontaneous speech). Initially, sounds should be introduced individually, in one position of the word (initial, medial, or final), and in 1-syllable words. As the client progresses, the instructor can quickly increase word length to 2-3 syllables, introduce other word positions, and target more than one sound in each trial.

Remember that some vowels are more difficult to produce in isolation, so starting with syllables or words may be easier. Also, some vowels do not occur in all positions of words. For example, /ɪ/ does not occur in the final position of words.

Table 4-8 below explains jaw height, lip rounding, and tongue placement for all vowels in GenAm as well as a description of how to produce the sound and common substitutions produced by accent modification clients.

References

Adapted from: Lexical Set. (2021, October 6). In Wikipedia. https://en.wikipedia.org/wiki/Lexical_set

<u>Table 4-8. Vowel Elicitation Techniques</u>

Sound	Jaw Height	Lip Rounding	Tongue Position	Elicitation Technique	Common Substitutions
/i/	Slight	Retracted	High/ Front	Slightly open your jaw, retract your lips, keep your tongue tense and towards the front of your mouth, turn your voice on and say 'e' or 'seat'	/ɪ/
/ɪ/	Slight	No	High/ Front	Slightly open your jaw, keep your lips relaxed, keep your tongue tense and towards the front of your mouth, turn your voice on and say 'ɪ' or 'sit'	/i/
/e/	Mid	No	Mid/ Front	Open your jaw to mid-level, keep your lips relaxed, keep your tongue slightly tense and towards the front of your mouth, turn your voice on and say 'a' or 'ate'	/ɛ/, /æ/
/ɛ/	Mid	No	Mid/ Front	Open your jaw to mid-level, keep your lips relaxed, keep your tongue tense and towards the front of your mouth, turn your voice on and say 'eh' or 'dress'	/e/, /ɪ/, /æ/
/æ/	Wide	No	Low/ Front	Open your jaw wide, keep your lips relaxed, keep your tongue relaxed and towards the front of your mouth, turn your voice on and say 'ae' or 'had'	/ɑ/, /ɛ/
/ɑ/	Wide	No	Low/ Front	Open your jaw wide, keep your lips relaxed, keep your tongue relaxed and towards the back of your mouth, turn your voice on and say 'ahh' or 'sock'	/æ/, /o/, /ə/
/ɔ/	Mid	Yes	Mid/ Back	Open your jaw to mid-level, round your lips, keep your tongue slightly tense and towards the back of your mouth, turn your voice on and say 'awe' or 'dog'	/o/

Sound	Jaw Height	Lip Rounding	Tongue Position	Elicitation Technique	Common Substitutions
/o/	Mid	Yes	Mid/ Back	Open your jaw to mid-level, round your lips, keep your tongue slightly tense and towards the b ack of your mouth, turn your voice on and say 'o' or 'coat'	/a/
/ʊ/	Slight	Yes	High/ Back	Open your jaw slightly, round your lips, keep your tongue tense and towards the back of your mouth, turn your voice on and say 'ʊ' or 'good'	/u/, /ə/
/u/	Slight	Yes	High/ Back	Open your jaw slightly, round your lips, keep your tongue tense and towards the back of your mouth, turn your voice on and say 'ooo' or 'boot'	/ʊ/
/ə, ʌ/	Mid	No	Mid/ Central	Open your jaw to mid-level, keep your lips relaxed, keep your tongue slightly tense and towards the middle of your mouth, turn your voice on and say 'uh' or 'cup'	/a/
/aɪ/ Diphthong	Wide-Slight	No	Low/Front-High/Front	Starting with your jaw open wide, lips relaxed, and tongue relaxed and towards the back of your mouth, move your jaw up so it is slightly open, tense up your tongue and bring it forward, turn your voice on and say 'I' or 'hi'	/a/, /ɪ/
/aʊ/ Diphthong	Wide-Slight	Yes	Low/Front-High/Back	Starting with your jaw open wide, lips rounded, and your tongue relaxed and up your tongue so that it is slightly open, tense up your tongue and bring it forward, turn your voice on and say 'ow' or 'cow'	/a/, /o/
/ɔɪ/ Diphthong	Mid-Slight	Yes/No	Mid/Back-High/Front	Starting with your jaw open to mid-level, lips rounded, and your tongue slightly tense and towards the back of your mouth, move your jaw up so that it is slightly open, tense up your tongue and bring it forward, relax your lips, turn your voice on and say 'oy' or 'toy'	/ɔ/, /ɪ/

Vowel Practice Stimuli

Because vowel stimuli are difficult to come across, I have included stimuli for each vowel sound in General American English (GenAm).

1. /e/ as in 'face'
2. /aʊ/ as in 'mouth'
3. /ɛ/ as in 'dress'
4. /i/ as in 'fleece'
5. /o/ as in 'goat'
6. /ɪ/ as in 'kit'
7. /æ/ as in 'trap'
8. /ʌ/ as in 'strut'
9. /a/ as in 'lot'
10. /ɔ/ as in 'thought'
11. /ʊ/ as in 'foot'
12. /u/ as in 'goose'
13. /ɔɪ/ as in 'choice'
14. /aɪ/ as in 'price'
15. Vocalic /ɹ/ as in 'nurse'

Each vowel set contains stimuli for the levels:

1. 105 single syllable words
2. 45 phrases with repeated occurrence of target
3. 105 phrases with a single occurrence of target
4. 40 sentences with repeated occurrence of target
5. 40 sentences with single occurrence of target

*The vowels /ɔ/ and /ʊ/ have fewer stimuli due to the decreased frequency of occurrence in GenAm.

Table 4-9a. Vowel: /e/						
Context: Word Level						
A	Name	Same	Tame	Came	Lame	Fame
Ate	Gate	Hate	Weight	Late	Wait	Date
Ace	Make	Cake	Shake	Take	Bake	Fake
Eight	Wake	Lake	Rake	Gape	Stay	Gray
Aim	Day	Lay	Pay	Say	Ray	Faye
Ache	May	Bay	Way	Rain	Braid	Made
Abe	Stayed	Blame	Game	Flame	Claim	Frame
Ale	Shame	Trade	James	Named	Pain	Paid
Aid	Jane	Weigh	Hey	Maid	Waste	Wade
Age	Hay	Prey	Spray	They	Tail	Slay
Nail	Jay	Play	Spay	Praise	Kay	Tray
Gain	Sway	Dave	Cave	Clay	Rail	Main
Page	Race	Wave	Bail	Base	Case	Haste
Stage	Lace	Place	Brain	Brace	Grade	Cape
Train	Chase	Gave	Fade	Fail	Break	Grape

Table 4-9b. Vowel: /e/		
Context: Phrase Level- Repeated Occurrence		
A place	Race wave	Blame maid
Named Jay	Say hey	Gray cape
May Day	Ache pain	Ate grape
Gave grade	Came late	Train rail
Bake cake	Hate stage	Haste waste
Main stay	Pay Wade	Break case
They made	Shake weight	Lame gate
Name Dave	Same page	Clay base
Claim fame	Lace frame	Date paid
Chase game	Take aim	Lake bay
Shame Jane	Rake hay	Fake cave
James stayed	Rain fail	Fade aid
Brain play	Make bail	Weigh eight
Braid tail	Flame ray	Tame prey
Wait, Abe	Aged ale	Brace sway

Table 4-9c. Vowel: /e/				
Context: Phrase Level- Single Occurrence				
A mouse	Your name	Same one	Tame animal	Came home
Ate lunch	Wooden gate	Don't hate	Lost weight	Late class
Ace card	Make a wish	Chocolate cake	Shake up	Take off
Eight years	Wake up	Smith Lake	Rake leaves	Gape hole
Aim high	Day one	Lay brick	Pay me	Say yes
Back ache	May I	Bay boat	This way	More rain
Call Abe	Stayed home	Blame him	New game	Big flame
Golden ale	Shame on you	Trade winds	Find James	Named her
First aid	Know Jane	Weigh in	Hey there	Hotel maid
Old age	Horse hay	Animal prey	Spray tan	They will
Nail gun	Blue Jay	Play time	Spay cat	Praise them
Gain more	Easy sway	With Dave	Bat cave	Clay pot
Page nine	Fast race	Big wave	Bail out	Home base
Stage fright	White lace	My place	My brain	Brace yourself
Train arrived	Chase down	Gave me	Fade out	Fail test
More fame	Next date	Fake purse	Gray vest	Know Faye
Not made	Picture frame	Paid off	Wade in water	Slay dragon
Lunch tray	Main one	Felt haste	Yellow cape	Eat grape
Was lame	Wait here	Bake cookies	Stay here	Sunshine ray
Braid hair	Did claim	Back pain	Food waste	Cat tail
Mary Kay	Rail tracks	This case	First grade	Spring break

Table 4-9d. Vowel: /e/	
Context: Sentence Level- Repeated Occurrence	
We played the same game in the rain.	Kay went sailing in the bay with Jane.
I will make a cake for the birthday in May.	Play the eighth ace to gain points.
Payne Lake has a gray bay.	Did you taste the aged grape flavor?
I can explain the crazy day.	The flame came from the gate.
They went to Trader Joes to taste the glaze.	James gave Jay a one-page note.
Tray has a place with a man cave.	The cat's tail and nail caused pain in my leg.
The maid was paid to make the bed.	I lay awake when things weigh on my mind.
The blame and shame were placed on Dave.	The wave made the clay dock sway.
The gray cape did not have a label.	They were late to class, so the grade was a fail.
The way to fame is to break a leg on stage.	You have to pay to take the train rail.
Haste makes waste is what they say.	The lady braids hair in Spain.
He claimed the name on the mail was Jay.	I got a pay raise for my main job.
The clay vase held its shape.	The praise was aimed to sway the judge.
Aches and pains are a part of age.	We will stay and wait for the train.
I will trade you the fake briefcase.	The date of the race is next May.
The tomato tastes like stale grapes.	Add lace to the frame to make it pretty.
The tame horse ate the hay bale.	Ray and Faye called to say hey!
I hate to make you wait if they are late.	The pay scale has a wide range.
I claimed my brain was playing tricks on me.	My brother Jake used to chase me with a rake.
We need first aid in case they are in pain.	The shake weight was the rage eight years ago.

Table 4-9e. Vowel: /e/	
Context: Sentence Level- Single Occurrence	
Is dinner at six or <u>eight</u>?	From what <u>gate</u> does our flight leave?
I want a big chocolate <u>cake</u>.	I use my <u>Chase</u> credit card for points.
He is my <u>ace</u> in the hole.	Please tell me your <u>name</u>.
Is this one the <u>same</u> or different?	I <u>hate</u> we missed you at the party.
The <u>game</u> will start at 5:30 p.m.	Can you show me the <u>way</u>?
Will you <u>pay</u> with cash or credit card?	I <u>raked</u> the leaves this weekend.
<u>Shake</u> up the salad dressing first.	You can <u>take</u> your turn next.
I was <u>late</u> for class because of snow.	Bread <u>came</u> with the soup and salad.
Please <u>wait</u> behind the line.	Where will you <u>stay</u> in Greece?
The picture <u>frame</u> is my mom's.	He <u>paid</u> me twenty dollars.
I <u>made</u> the pie from scratch.	The kids will <u>play</u> outside.
She loves to <u>bake</u> cookies.	The <u>date</u> of the exam is tomorrow.
This vendor sells <u>fake</u> purses.	Put this in the <u>waste</u> basket.
The hotel <u>maid</u> is here to clean.	We <u>ate</u> lunch and dinner out.
My back <u>ache</u> is getting worse.	What time did you <u>wake</u> up this morning?
Will you <u>make</u> me a sandwich?	The <u>sway</u> bridge is very scary.
My hair <u>spray</u> is the super hold.	Where is the first <u>aid</u> kit?
At what <u>age</u> can you vote?	I just broke my finger <u>nail</u>.
It's a <u>race</u> to the finish line.	It is supposed to <u>rain</u> all night.
I need a <u>break</u> from work.	The <u>grape</u> rolled under the table.

Table 4-10a. Vowel: /aʊ/						
Context: Word Level						
Ow	Bow	Cow	How	Wow	Now	Pow
Ouch	Clown	Brow	Plow	Town	Ounce	Vow
Out	Thou	Vouch	Chow	Cowl	Bout	Frown
Owl	Brown	Foul	Howl	Prowl	Jowl	Yowl
Oust	Cows	Browse	Plows	Scowls	Vows	Frowns
Hour	Wowed	Plowed	Scowled	Vowed	Fouls	Howls
Prowls	Mouth	Down	Gouge	Douse	Fouled	Scout
Scouts	Shout	Bowed	Doubt	Shouts	Touts	Doubts
Drought	Route	Clout	Droughts	Stout	Laos	Snout
Sprout	Grout	Clouts	Rouse	Snouts	Sprouts	Kraut
Noun	Count	Mount	Trout	South	Counts	Mounts
Tout	Couch	Bows	Slouch	Blouse	Growl	Slouched
Sound	Tao	Loud	Proud	Cloud	Crowd	House
Pound	Crowds	Gown	Sour	Bound	Browned	Crown
Ground	Round	Found	Frowned	Mouse	Drown	Spout

Table 4-10b. Vowel: /aʊ/		
Context: Phrase Level- Repeated Occurrence		
Brown couch	Sprout kraut	Bowed down
Yowl howl	Browned trout	Slouched around
Clown snout	Owl yowled	Wow pow
Wowed crowd	Tout Tao	Found house
Jowl frown	Drought cloud	Route bound
Count doubts	Browse town	Grouch slouch
Mount grout	Down spout	Oust out
Ow ouch	Shout out	Loud crowds
How now	Plows sprouts	Scowl brow
Shouts loud	Bout doubt	Chow Chow
Proud foul	Stout clout	Scout prowl
Scowls frowns	Fouled vows	Vowed fouls
Cow snouts	South touts	Sound howls
Scouts prowled	Thou crown	Plowed routes
Counts blouse	Bow down	Cows growl

Table 4-10c. Vowel: /aʊ/				
Context: Phrase Level- Single Occurrence				
Ow that hurt	Boat bow	Spotted cow	How so	Oh wow
Big ouch	Funny clown	Wiped brow	Plow field	Small town
Leaving town	Thou art	Vouch for me	Chow mein	Cowl neck
Big owl	Brown shirt	Foul ball	Dog howl	Prowl sales
Oust him	Cows fence	Browse store	Buy plows	He scowls
One hour	Wowed me	Plowed field	She scowled	He vowed
Animal prowls	Big mouth	Sit down	It prowled	Douse pizza
Boy scouts	Don't shout	He bowed	In doubt	He shouts
Water drought	Route 1	More clout	Few droughts	Is stout
Green sprout	Tub grout	It clouts	Rouse up	Dog snouts
Use noun	Count on	Mount picture	Caught trout	Deep south
Much tout	Red couch	Boat bows	Don't slouch	Nice blouse
No sound	Written Tao	Loud people	Proud of	Dark cloud
Lobster pound	Big crowds	Silk gown	Sour fruit	Italy bound
Leaps & bounds	Round shape	Lost and found	He frowned	Crowned king
Not now	Big pow	Sport fouls	Wolf howls	That counts
One ounce	Say vow	Was fouled	Girl scout	Cat growl
Long bout	Big frown	She touts	More doubts	Holiday crowd
Hog jowl	Big yowl	Visit Laos	Pig snout	Browned butter
Said vows	No frowns	Bean sprouts	Very sour	May drown
The mounts	Was slouched	The house	Royal crown	Water spout

Table 4-10d. Vowel: /aʊ/	
Context: Sentence Level- Repeated Occurrence	
You can <u>mount</u> the <u>grout</u> on the boat <u>bow</u>.	He <u>howled</u> <u>ow</u>, <u>ouch</u>, that hurt!
The <u>crowd</u> is <u>shouting</u> <u>loudly</u>.	He <u>slouched</u> <u>down</u> on his <u>brown</u> <u>couch</u>.
Do <u>sows</u> or <u>cows</u> <u>growl</u>?	The royal <u>crown</u> <u>wowed</u> the <u>crowd</u>.
The <u>owl</u> let <u>out</u> a <u>yowl</u> and <u>howl</u>.	Have you tried the <u>browned</u> <u>trout</u> with <u>sprouts</u>?
It's <u>about</u> time for a <u>shout-out</u>.	Take the one-<u>hour</u> <u>route</u> to <u>town</u>.
<u>Down</u> <u>south</u>, they take <u>vows</u> seriously.	<u>Clowns</u> can't <u>frown</u> or <u>scowl</u>.
I was on the <u>prowl</u> and <u>found</u> a <u>cowl</u> neck shirt.	The <u>mouse</u> in the <u>house</u> has a <u>spouse</u>.
I wore a <u>gown</u> <u>out</u> on the <u>town</u>.	The <u>loud</u> <u>howl</u> <u>aroused</u> the sleeping boy.
Put <u>sauerkraut</u> on the <u>browned</u> <u>sprouts</u>.	The <u>louse</u> on the <u>grouse</u> was <u>found</u>.
<u>Sow</u> <u>jowls</u> are better <u>browned</u>.	Her <u>brown</u> <u>brows</u> were <u>scowling</u>.
We <u>browsed</u> the <u>town</u> for <u>flour</u>.	The <u>joust</u> lost his <u>crown</u> because of a <u>foul</u>.
The <u>owl</u> is on the <u>prowl</u> for a <u>mouse</u>.	The boy <u>scouts</u> are <u>proud</u> of their <u>clout</u>.
We can <u>lounge</u> on the <u>round</u> <u>couch</u>.	We are <u>bound</u> for <u>Laos</u> on the fastest <u>route</u>.
The <u>joust</u> took a <u>vow</u> for the <u>crown</u>.	Take the <u>flower</u> <u>out</u> of the vase <u>now</u>.
<u>Count</u> the <u>owls</u> in the <u>clouds</u>.	Can you <u>count</u> <u>aloud</u> for an <u>hour</u>?
I <u>found</u> a <u>flower</u> in the <u>house</u>.	<u>Our</u> <u>trout</u> pond is <u>down</u> there.
<u>Count</u> the <u>brown</u> and white <u>cows</u>.	The <u>clown</u> is <u>outside</u> <u>now</u>.
The <u>fowl</u> are <u>bound</u> for the <u>south</u>.	The <u>brown</u> <u>stout</u> is <u>cloudy</u>.
The <u>Chow</u> <u>Chow</u> got <u>out</u> of the yard.	I <u>shouted</u> when I saw the <u>mouse</u> in the <u>pouch</u>.
<u>Wow</u>, <u>how</u> will you get <u>down</u> from there?	The <u>town's</u> best <u>chowder</u> is in the <u>tower</u>.

Table 4-10e. Vowel: /aʊ/
Context: Sentence Level- Single Occurrence

The Grinch is a <u>grouch</u>.	<u>Ouch,</u> you stepped on my toe!
Don't <u>crowd</u> the doorway, please.	<u>How</u> are you doing today?
The cat is on the <u>prowl</u> for dinner.	The <u>endowment</u> is one million dollars.
Do you like <u>Sprouts</u> or Whole Foods?	The water <u>spout</u> is not leaking.
The dark <u>clouds</u> look ominous.	It's <u>about</u> time we go home.
We are <u>out</u> of salt and sugar.	We need <u>flour</u> for the cake.
I can <u>vouch</u> for her.	Winfield is a sleepy little <u>town</u>.
He should shut his <u>mouth</u>.	The <u>South</u> is hot and humid.
Please go <u>around</u> the spilled water.	They will <u>allow</u> you to go.
The <u>brown</u> dog is named Harley.	<u>Our</u> favorite show is Breaking Bad.
We need a <u>noun</u> and adjective.	They did <u>count</u> all of the votes.
Sit <u>down</u> in the red chair.	<u>Now</u> is not the time.
Take <u>Route</u> 1 to Key West.	The <u>cows</u> are in the pasture.
The <u>crown</u> jewels are on display in London.	They are very <u>proud</u> parents.
Have you read the entire <u>Tao</u>?	The wedding <u>gown</u> needs to be altered.
He has a big <u>frown</u> on his face.	I like to <u>douse</u> my pizza in ranch dressing.
They <u>gouge</u> prices before holidays.	Do you prefer <u>trout</u> or salmon?
There is a <u>drought</u> every summer.	I <u>doubt</u> we will be traveling soon.
The fans like to <u>shout</u> at the team.	Brussel <u>sprouts</u> are pretty popular.
We are <u>bound</u> for the championship!	I <u>found</u> twenty dollars today.

Table 4-11a. Vowel: /ɛ/						
Context: Word Level						
Egg	Net	Fell	Guess	Ned	Zen	Spent
Elk	Neck	Bell	Mess	Ted	Speck	Vest
Edge	Den	Tell	Bless	Gem	Mend	Shed
Ed	Lend	Sell	Less	Yes	Spend	Sled
Bed	Peck	Smell	Rest	Sweat	Blend	Stem
Beg	Check	Deck	Guest	Hem	Shell	Gel
Less	Pen	Red	Leg	Yell	Swell	Fleck
Yet	Send	Head	Test	Ken	Best	Bread
Let	Cent	Said	Pest	Yep	Zest	Step
Best	Wreck	Set	Help	Rest	West	Fret
Men	Then	Bet	Belt	Prep	Jest	Quell
Ten	Jet	Get	Felt	Jeff	Lest	Pledge
Hen	When	Met	Melt	Vet	Web	Best
Bend	Sent	Debt	Well	Peg	Wed	Led
Pet	End	Wet	Dead	Fed	Vent	Went

Table 4-11b. Vowel: /ɛ/		
Context: Phrase Level- Repeated Occurrence		
Ten cents	Smell pet	Fleck melt
Crest swell	Pest mess	Bread zest
Mend belt	Wet head	Send check
Rest guest	Blend well	Met Ned
Men den	Spend less	Wed Ted
Egg shell	Test prep	Went West
Red gem	Sell bells	Best guess
Sled shed	Tell Ken	Get set
Let rest	Bet debt	Jet wreck
Yell help	Bed peg	Yet vent
Elk vet	Said yes	Dead end
Then when	Hem vest	Bend stem
Gent Jeff	Hen peck	Leg gel
Ed fell	Felt Zen	Quell fret
Sweat less	Deck edge	Pledge sent

		Table 4-11c. Vowel: /ɛ/		
		Context: Phrase Level- Single Occurrence		
Egg bite	Fish net	I fell	Guess what	Know Ned
Saw elk	Giraffe neck	Ring bell	Big mess	Call Ted
Ford Edge	Dark den	Do tell	Bless you	Hide gem
Know Ed	Will lend	Did sell	Costs less	Maybe yes
New bed	Little peck	Bad smell	Need rest	More sweat
Don't beg	Write check	Wood deck	House guest	Hem skirt
More or less	Blue pen	Color red	Hurt leg	Yell loudly
Not yet	Hit send	Big head	Take test	Call Ken
Let me know	One cent	She said	The pest	Yep, it is
Best one	Train wreck	All set	Need help	Just rest
Group of men	Well sure	Place bet	Seat belt	Food prep
Count to ten	Jet pack	Get up	Felt smooth	Visit Jeff
Big hen	Is when	Met up	Snow melt	Called vet
Bend, Oregon	Just sent	Bad debt	Well done	Wood peg
Pet dog	The end	All wet	Dead battery	Fed meal
Feel Zen	Money spent	Found shell	Hair gel	In jest
Small speck	New vest	Just swell	Gold fleck	Lest he worries
Mend pants	Blue shed	Best man	Bread stick	Spider web
Spend more	Round sled	Orange zest	Side step	Did wed
Coffee blend	Flower stem	Go West	Don't fret	Vent to me
Quell worries	Made pledge	Best one	Was led	Went there

Table 4-11d. Vowel: /ɛ/
Context: Sentence Level- Repeated Occurrence

The <u>bells</u> are <u>ten</u> <u>cents</u> each.	I <u>met</u> <u>Ned</u> at the <u>breakfast</u> buffet.
The <u>fleck</u> of snow <u>melted</u> on my <u>vest</u>.	I <u>mended</u> the <u>felt</u> <u>belt</u>.
The <u>eggshell</u> <u>fell</u> in the <u>bread</u>.	Please <u>send</u> the <u>check</u> to <u>Ted</u>.
We hit a <u>dead</u>-<u>end</u> in the <u>jet</u>.	We need to <u>let</u> <u>Ken</u> <u>rest</u>.
The <u>guest</u> <u>set</u> out <u>West</u>.	We <u>went</u> to <u>get</u> <u>help</u>.
My <u>best</u> <u>guess</u> is <u>yes</u>.	They <u>sell</u> <u>red</u> <u>gems</u> there.
The <u>shed</u> <u>vent</u> has a <u>smell</u>.	<u>Jeff</u> and <u>Ed</u> <u>fell</u> in the <u>den</u>.
You <u>sweat</u> <u>less</u> if you <u>rest</u> <u>well</u>.	The <u>bent</u> flower <u>stem</u> had a <u>gem</u>.
<u>Get</u> <u>set</u> to <u>head</u> <u>West</u>.	To make <u>bread,</u> you must <u>blend</u> <u>well</u>.
The <u>ten</u> <u>elk</u> caused a <u>wreck</u>.	I need <u>gel</u> for my <u>leg</u> from the <u>hen</u> <u>peck</u>.
The <u>test</u> <u>prep</u> is on <u>Wednesday</u>.	He <u>said</u> his <u>debt</u> is from a lost <u>bet</u>.
After yoga on <u>Wednesday,</u> I <u>felt</u> <u>Zen</u>.	<u>Let</u> the <u>rest</u> of us <u>help</u> you.
The <u>sleds</u> are in the <u>red</u> <u>shed</u>.	My <u>pet</u> was such a <u>pest</u> and <u>left</u> a <u>mess</u>.
If you <u>spend</u> <u>less,</u> you can <u>get</u> rid of <u>debt</u>.	I <u>sent</u> in my <u>pledge</u> with my <u>check</u>.
There are <u>ten</u> <u>hens</u> in the <u>den</u>.	I hit my <u>neck</u> on the <u>edge</u> of the <u>deck</u>.
<u>Jeff</u> is a <u>med</u> <u>student</u> in <u>debt</u>.	I need to <u>mend</u> the <u>hem</u> of my <u>vest</u>.
<u>Ned</u> <u>said</u> the joke in <u>jest</u>.	The <u>web</u> has a <u>pest</u>, so the spider will be <u>fed</u>.
The <u>best</u>-<u>kept</u> secret is 'less is more.'	Can you <u>lend</u> me a <u>red</u> <u>pen</u>?
The <u>wet</u> <u>Swell</u> bottle <u>left</u> a ring of <u>sweat</u>.	The <u>deck</u> <u>step</u> needs a new <u>peg</u>.
If not <u>Wednesday,</u> <u>then</u> <u>when</u>?	I <u>sent</u> the <u>best</u> <u>message</u> to <u>friends</u> with <u>zest</u>!

Table 4-11e. Vowel: /ɛ/	
Context: Sentence Level- Single Occurrence	
There was a <u>speck</u> of dust on the floor.	The <u>shed</u> needs a new roof.
The flower <u>stem</u> is green.	The blue <u>pen</u> leaked on the paper.
My bike wheel <u>fell</u> off.	I will <u>spend</u> the week with my parents.
My <u>friends</u> are in class.	He needs to <u>rest</u> more!
Do these chips have a strange <u>smell</u>?	My <u>guess</u> is she will go.
I hit my <u>leg</u> on the table.	The <u>best</u> holiday is July 4.
The car <u>wreck</u> was minor.	We need milk and 1 <u>egg</u> for the cookies.
There are lots of <u>elk</u> in the park.	I bought a new green <u>vest</u>.
The Ford <u>Edge</u> is a nice car.	Did he say <u>yes</u> or no?
Have you been out <u>West</u>?	I will be <u>next</u> door to you.
I found one <u>cent</u> on the sidewalk.	Don't <u>yell</u> at the other team.
This week is super <u>hectic</u> for me.	You will need <u>less</u> than you think.
He will <u>tell</u> the story.	They are trying to <u>sell</u> the house.
My teacher <u>said</u> there was homework.	<u>Ted</u> is running another marathon.
The turtle <u>shell</u> looks old.	Can you <u>help</u> me move this?
I asked him to be my <u>best</u> man.	The <u>mess</u> from the party needs to be cleaned.
I always <u>spend</u> more than I should.	My dog will <u>beg</u> for a treat.
I will <u>let</u> you decide which one.	I have a big <u>headache</u>.
The movie starts at <u>ten</u> p.m.	I <u>bet</u> he will buy the car.
<u>When</u> is the birthday brunch?	The hair <u>gel</u> is super sticky.

Table 4-12a. Vowel: /i/						
Context: Word Level						
Eel	Cheap	Feet	Jeep	Peach	Seen	Sweet
Eat	Cheat	Feed	Keep	Peak	She	Tea
Eek	Chief	Field	Key	Peel	Sheep	Teach
Be	Clean	Flee	Lead	Peep	Sheet	Team
Bead	Creak	Free	Leak	Piece	Sleek	The
Beach	Cream	Freeze	Leap	Plead	Sleep	Three
Beak	Creep	Gleam	Leave	Reach	Sneak	Treat
Beam	Deal	Glee	Me	Read	Sneeze	Tree
Bean	Dean	Green	Meal	Real	Speech	Teen
Beast	Dear	Greet	Mean	Screen	Speak	We
Beat	Deed	Grief	Meet	Sea	Steep	Week
Beep	Deem	He	Neat	Seat	Streak	Weep
Bleed	Deep	Heal	Need	Seed	Stream	Wheat
Breeze	Dream	Heat	Niece	Seek	Street	Weed
Brief	Fee	Jeans	Pea	Seem	Sweep	Weave

Table 4-12b. Vowel: /i/		
Context: Phrase Level- Repeated Occurrence		
Sea eel	Real cheap	Teen week
Eat meat	Field pea	Sweet tea
Shriek eek	Dear chief	We feed
Be mean	Clean screen	Free speech
Teal bead	Deep heat	Heal feet
Beach breeze	Peach cream	Meet me
Seek sheep	Sneak sleep	Key piece
Peak beam	Wheat seed	Sleek reach
Green bean	Weak tree	Cheat sheet
Greet beast	Speech sneeze	Creaky plead
Feel beat	Steep deed	Teach niece
Deep beep	Team three	Stream freeze
Lead bleed	Neat meal	Grief streak
Sweep street	Dream read	Keep Jeep
Brief fee	Need peace	Gleam glee

Table 4-12c. Vowel: /i/				
Context: Phrase Level- Single Occurrence				
Big eel	Dirt cheap	Two feet	New Jeep	Peach pit
Should eat	Don't cheat	Just feed	Keep it	Pike's Peak
Oh eek	New chief	Football field	Key West	Peel shrimp
Be careful	Should clean	Will flee	Project lead	Little Bo Peep
One bead	Floor creak	Is free	Water leak	Piece of cake
Nice beach	Shaving cream	Cold freeze	Leap frog	To plead
Bird beak	Loud creep	Bright gleam	Leave it	Reach it
Balance beam	Good deal	Glee club	Pick me	Read book
Lima bean	New Dean	Color green	Great meal	Real time
A beast	Dear friend	Greet guests	Was mean	Bug screen
Drum beat	House deed	Good grief	Meet her	Red Sea
Car beep	Was deemed	He can	Neat plan	Seat belt
Did bleed	Deep hole	Can heal	Need one	Flower seed
Nice breeze	Bad dream	More heat	My niece	Hide and seek
New brief	High fee	Blue jeans	Snow pea	Does seem
Not seen	Sweet pie	Sleep well	Three times	Steep hill
She did	Iced tea	Will sneak	Trick or treat	Wild streak
White sheep	Teach them	Big sneeze	Pine tree	Long stream
Warm sheet	Football team	Great speech	Teen clothes	Main street
Sleek hair	Mean group	Did speak	We were	Sweep up
First week	Don't weep	Wheat thins	Little weed	Basket weave

Table 4-12d. Vowel: /i/
*In connected speech, the vowel in 'the' is typically reduced to a schwa. Therefore, it is not underlined below
Context: Sentence Level- Repeated Occurrence

The peach pit seemed sweet.

Meat, cheese, and tea are in the evening.

The team will keep the Jeep.

She does like a deal on sweet tea.

Leave me alone before my big test.

The sleek piece of the Jeep fell free.

The eel will reach the green sea.

I had a dream about a tree in the street.

The sleek bird beak has a gleam.

We will eat in the creek for a fee.

Eek, my dry heel needs cream.

The brief breeze was neat and clean.

We must weed the green grass by the stream.

The brief beep means it is time to meet.

We can email the brief this evening.

The free movie screen will stream later.

The seat by the sea is cheap.

The teal tweed matches my jeans.

The wheat will be deemed ready to yield.

I can teach Gene to seek his dream.

The mean sea is big and green.

He did read the speech by the tree.

He will speak and then sleep by the stream.

The neat stream will freeze in pieces.

The breezy sea can reach the steep sidewalk.

Meet me in Key West to greet Sheila.

He did read the real speech.

The pink jeans were really cheap.

Sweet tea is steeped in a field.

We must sneak a brief sleep.

The sweet niece doesn't make a peep.

The team will plant the tree seed.

The fee for Pike's Peak is very steep.

The Dean made a deal with the team.

He feels like he has two left feet.

There is a fee to see the sleek sheep.

My dream is a real reach.

The weak speech was very mean.

The zebra has a sweet zeal.

We seem to cheat sleep to study.

Table 4-12e. Vowel: /i/	
Context: Sentence Level- Single Occurrence	
There is a high <u>fee</u> for this.	I had a bad <u>dream</u>.
Do you <u>sleep</u> with the fan on?	One <u>sheep</u> got over the fence.
My bike <u>wheel</u> fell off.	<u>Dean</u> Smith is new to Gallaudet.
I want to <u>eat</u> right now.	Ice <u>cream</u> is my favorite snack.
I will <u>speak</u> to him.	Jane likes sugar with her <u>tea</u>.
<u>Key</u> West is just perfect!	This <u>tweed</u> jacket is new.
Blake did <u>read</u> the news report.	This fall, our football <u>team</u> won.
I like holidays for the <u>treats</u>.	A <u>bead</u> fell off my bracelet.
Pike's <u>Peak</u> is in Colorado.	Julia was so <u>sweet</u> to Ben!
What a <u>neat</u> trick that was!	I will <u>be</u> there for you.
First, <u>peel</u> the carrots for dinner.	<u>Glee</u> club is today at 5:00 a.m.
This <u>week</u> is super hectic for you.	<u>He</u> knows Shar very well.
That was very <u>mean</u> of you!	Their winning <u>streak</u> is over.
A basketball <u>team</u> just showed up.	You should <u>greet</u> the guests.
<u>Please</u> go to the store.	<u>Green</u> is not a good color on you.
Did you <u>read</u> his new book?	That loud <u>beep</u> was the car alarm.
My <u>feet</u> are cold and sore.	I can <u>peel</u> more shrimp for lunch.
There is a water <u>leak</u> in Gelman.	<u>Leave</u> Alex alone right now!
It is an all-you-can-<u>eat</u> buffet.	Bryan's <u>Jeep</u> is not working.
There is a <u>freeze</u> warning tonight.	I will <u>clean</u> it up after class.

Table 4-13a. Vowel: /o/						
Context: Word Level						
Oh	Row	Boat	Poach	Soap	Groan	Toast
Oat	Croak	Bloat	Snow	Bow	Bone	No
Owe	Pro	Go	Goat	Stow	Dough	Dote
Own	Low	Though	Toe	So	Know	Toad
Ode	Tow	Sew	Slow	Blow	Glow	Crow
Oak	Yo	Hoe	Pose	Froze	Close	Those
Flown	Rose	Nose	Clothes	Chose	Grow	Hose
Foes	Woes	Doze	Moe	Joe	Owes	Bose
Co	Mow	Robe	Globe	Poke	Broke	Road
Soak	Loaf	Comb	Rode	Home	Phone	Stone
Zone	Rome	Note	Wrote	Stove	Vote	Jokes
Roam	Loam	Moat	Float	Gloat	Tote	Tone
Drone	Sloan	Mode	Flow	Whoa	Loan	Woke
Foe	Bro	Load	Coat	Rote	Bo	Bode
Moan	Cone	Show	Oath	Bloke	Foam	Gnome

Table 4-13b. Vowel: /o/		
Context: Phrase Level- Repeated Occurrence		
Road show	Soak zone	Float boat
Wrote note	Nose bone	Go slow
Load toast	Stove loaf	Roam globe
Broke phone	Owe Joe	Chose coat
Grow goats	Stow glow	Close hose
Knows foes	Stone moat	Rote mode
Froze toe	Blow snow	So though
Know Bo	Own drone	Oh no
Poke Moe	Tote those	Mow rose
Toad croak	Bro jokes	Sew clothes
Poach soap	Low row	Yo foe
Bose Co	Whoa crow	Doze robe
Flow pose	Rode vote	Tone gloat
Oak hoe	Oat dough	Moan groan
Flown home	Bode woes	Comb foam

Table 4-13c. Vowel: /o/				
Context: Phrase Level- Single Occurrence				
Oh my	Row faster	New boat	Poach eggs	Bar of soap
Oat milk	Croak loud	Feel bloat	Snow pile	Tie bow
Owe money	Pro athlete	Go soon	Goat farm	Stow above
Own it	Low battery	Though we may	Stub toe	So what
Ode to him	Tow the car	Sew a button	Slow down	Blow away
Flown first class	Yo I'm here	Wooden hoe	New pose	Pipes froze
Oak tree	Rose petal	Plug nose	Winter clothes	Chose that
Friend and foes	My woes	Doze off	Named Moe	Call Joe
Alex and Co	Mow the yard	Cotton robe	Travel globe	Poke me
Soak feet	Loaf of bread	Comb hair	Rode by	Went home
Quiet zone	Rome, Italy	Left a note	Wrote letter	Stove top
Roam around	Loam soil	A moat	Will float	Does gloat
Fly drone	Call Sloan	Silent mode	Water flow	Whoa now
Common foe	Baby bro	Truck load	Need coat	Rote memory
Low moan	Traffic cone	Great show	Take an oath	Nice bloke
Loud groan	Made toast	Close door	Those are mine	Vote now
Break bone	Said no	Grow flower	Hose off	Tote bag
Cookie dough	Dote on me	Owes money	Bose speakers	Need loan
I know him	Green toad	Broke down	Long road	Bo Jackson
Light glow	Black crow	New phone	Big stone	Foam mattress
Play jokes	Tone muscle	Woke up	Bode well	A gnome

Table 4-13d. Vowel: /o/	
Context: Sentence Level- Repeated Occurrence	
I <u>vote</u> for <u>goat</u> <u>yoga</u>.	I use <u>oat</u> milk in my <u>oatmeal</u> on the <u>stove</u>.
<u>Oprah</u> <u>owns</u> her <u>own</u> network.	The <u>gopher's</u> <u>home</u> is <u>over</u> there.
I <u>wrote</u> a <u>poem</u> in the <u>note</u>.	The <u>snow</u> <u>cone</u> has a red <u>glow</u>.
I'm a <u>stone's</u> <u>throw</u> away from <u>home</u>.	There was an <u>ode</u> to <u>Bo</u> Jackson in <u>Rome</u>.
I <u>almost</u> <u>froze</u> my <u>toes</u> in the <u>snow</u>.	<u>Joe</u> and I want to <u>go</u> around the <u>globe</u>.
I said <u>no,</u> <u>although</u> I took an <u>oath</u>.	<u>Moe</u> can <u>grow</u> beautiful <u>roses</u>.
Put the <u>dough</u> in the <u>stove,</u> <u>so</u> it can <u>grow</u>.	My <u>phone</u> in my <u>tote</u> just <u>broke</u>.
If you <u>roam</u> through a <u>moat,</u> you will get <u>soaked</u>.	The <u>snow</u> <u>blower</u> is near the <u>road</u>.
My favorite <u>yoga</u> <u>pose</u> is to <u>doze</u>.	The water in the <u>hose</u> <u>froze</u> in the <u>snow</u>.
We have a <u>GoPro</u> for the <u>drone</u>.	<u>Those</u> are <u>poached</u> eggs and <u>oat</u> milk.
We <u>floated</u> and <u>roamed</u> around the <u>oak</u> trees.	Will the <u>boat</u> <u>float</u> in the <u>moat</u>?
The <u>dough</u> will be a bread <u>loaf,</u> then <u>toast</u>.	The <u>rose</u> <u>robe</u> is <u>owned</u> by the <u>hotel</u>.
<u>Joe</u> <u>owes</u> his <u>foes</u> more money.	I <u>broke</u> a <u>bone</u> in my <u>toe</u>.
<u>Oh</u>, we took an <u>oath</u> before the <u>show</u>.	<u>Go</u> <u>slowly</u> in the <u>no</u>-wake <u>zone</u>.
<u>Rose</u> can <u>sew</u> <u>clothes</u> for you.	The crowd <u>moaned</u> and <u>groaned</u> at the <u>jokes</u>.
<u>Oh</u> <u>no</u>, please <u>slow</u> down!	<u>Load</u> the <u>toast</u> in the <u>stove</u>.
I will <u>go</u> <u>home</u> to get my <u>coat</u>.	<u>Stow</u> the <u>drone</u> near the <u>road</u>.
<u>Joe</u> <u>moaned</u> when the dog <u>woke</u> him up.	Put the <u>phone</u> on <u>slow</u> <u>mode</u>.
I <u>know</u> not to <u>gloat</u> before I <u>vote</u>.	The <u>stone</u> <u>road</u> is in a <u>flood</u> <u>zone</u>.
The <u>rowboat</u> needs a <u>tow</u>.	<u>Go</u> get <u>soap</u> and <u>soak</u> your feet.

Table 4-13e. Vowel: /o/	
Context: Sentence Level- Single Occurrence	
<u>Oh</u>, he will be here soon!	Do you want a <u>poached</u> egg for breakfast?
We need <u>soap</u> and water.	The jam is for the <u>toast</u>.
I <u>owe</u> you some money.	I was in the <u>zone</u>.
My <u>robe</u> is soft and comfy.	The <u>drone</u> flew above the roof.
The <u>loaf</u> of bread is wheat.	Do you use a <u>comb</u> or brush?
Be sure to <u>vote</u> today!	It will <u>snow</u> on Tuesday morning.
The <u>oak</u> tree may fall.	There is <u>no</u> way I can get there.
We visited <u>Rome</u>, Italy in the fall.	I forgot to turn off the <u>stove</u>.
The meeting is in the <u>rose</u> garden.	The pipes <u>froze</u> in the ice.
This news will <u>blow</u> up my media page.	<u>Those</u> are the ones I was looking for.
I have a new <u>phone</u> now.	Grandmas love to <u>dote</u> on their grandkids.
The cookie <u>dough</u> is in the freezer.	The flower <u>show</u> is this afternoon.
Milly <u>grows</u> award-winning flowers.	Please <u>close</u> the door behind you.
I do <u>know</u> what you mean.	The <u>glow</u> from the candle is dim.
I will <u>soak</u> my feet in warm water.	We will <u>roam</u> around the new city.
The truck <u>load</u> is too heavy.	Can you put it on silent <u>mode</u>?
We need a <u>float</u> for the pool.	I <u>wrote</u> the paper at 2:00 a.m.
He <u>rode</u> the train to the airport.	<u>Home</u> is where the heart is.
Make a right into the <u>stone</u> driveway.	I <u>own</u> two horses and one mule.
I prefer <u>oat</u> milk, not almond.	The bread <u>loaf</u> is fresh.

Table 4-14a. Vowel: /ɪ/						
Context: Word Level						
It	Bit	Fin	Kit	Bill	Mitt	Hid
Ill	Rip	Sit	Dim	Lit	Quit	Rid
Is	Tim	Fit	Lick	Bib	Kick	Sick
In	Did	Jig	Kid	Lid	Big	Dig
Its	Hill	Pill	Still	Grill	Him	Pick
If	Win	Hip	Lip	Sip	Zip	Tip
Miss	Give	Live	Pig	Grin	Dip	Fig
Kin	Pin	Bin	Tin	Rim	Hit	Wit
Fib	Brick	Chill	Crib	Drill	Fill	Fish
Fix	Flip	Wig	Grip	Itch	Rib	Knit
List	Rig	Mix	Quick	Ship	Thin	Sin
Six	Spill	Thick	Whip	Blip	Limp	Tick
Blimp	Wick	Shrimp	Trish	Trim	Slim	Pinch
Inch	Flinch	Grit	Gill	Skit	Gin	Skid
Brit	Pit	Zit	Spit	Slit	Flick	This

Table 4-14b. Vowel: /ɪ/		
Context: Phrase Level- Repeated Occurrence		
Is Brit	Fish fin	Pick six
Fig dip	Lip grin	Big mitt
Kick him	Grill shrimp	Give fib
Kiss Tim	Fix this	Sick pig
Dim lit	Quit it	Quick tip
Ship skiff	Still itch	Drill fill
Whip mix	Rig spill	Hit rim
Thin chin	Dig in	Did win
Chill pill	Kill Bill	Miss kin
Thick grip	Hip jig	Tin bin
Rip list	Whiz kid	Knit pin
Brick tin	Slim trim	Sip lid
Blip glitch	Flip wig	Hid wit
If it's	Ill Tim	Skid hill
Pinch rib	Crib bib	Blimp tick

		Table 4-14c. Vowel: /ɪ/		
		Context: Phrase Level- Single Occurrence		
It can	Bit hard	See fin	First aid kit	Know Bill
Felt ill	Rip up	Sit down	Dim light	Lit candle
Is not	Know Tim	Feel fit	Lick batter	Big baby
Not in	Did what	A jig	My kid	Closed lid
Its own	Steep hill	Take pill	Still not	Hot grill
What if	Win game	Hurt hip	Lip gloss	Take a sip
Miss you	Give back	Will try	Pig pen	Show grin
Next of kin	Jeweled pin	Trash bin	Tin can	Tire rim
Tell a fib	Brick lane	Felt chill	New crib	Need drill
Fix up	Flip house	Lost wig	Get a grip	Does itch
Grocery list	Oil rig	Mix up	Quick bite	Cargo ship
Six more	Big one	Thick hair	Cool whip	Small blip
Red blimp	Candle wick	Jumbo shrimp	Like Trish	Trim tree
Grew an inch	Don't flinch	True grit	The gill	Short skit
Know Brit	Fire pit	New zit	Bike spin	Cut slit
Oven mitt	Hid there	Zip up	Leave a tip	Looks thin
Just quit	Rid of	Veggie dip	Fig tree	Go limp
Kick down	Felt sick	Direct hit	Use wit	Slim down
Big one	Dig hole	Fill up	Caught fish	Gin and juice
Show him	Pick one	Poke rib	To knit	Flick off
The sin	Found tick	Pinch me	Car skid	This one

Table 4-14d. Vowel: /ɪ/	
Context: Sentence Level- Repeated Occurrence	
Is Tim a Brit or Italian?	The kickoff was a pick-six.
It's a quick tip for you.	The rig had a big oil spill.
Bill is a whiz kid.	Can you bring me the big mitt for the grill?
Kim quickly felt ill after dinner.	My Fitbit has a glitch.
The shrimp and fig dips are delicious.	The ball hit the rim and then went in.
Kill Bill is a movie that will win awards.	Will will flip his lid when he finds out.
I miss my friend Jim and his kids.	If it's cold, the candle wick will be lit.
The tennis team did win the jig.	We will rig something up to fix this.
The little boy will give a fib.	Take a sip from the open lid before it spills.
The ship has a painted slim trim.	He made them laugh with his quick wit.
The sick pig will live on the farm.	Don't ignore the quick tip.
He needs a chill pill for it.	There was a big blip and glitch in the data.
Mix the Cool Whip with the figs for a dip.	The baby's bib in the crib was thin.
The thick quilt needed a new stitch.	We should fill the kit with pins.
Please fix this quickly for him!	Pinch me so I know if it's true.
Dig into the big list and get started.	The ship's skiff looks very hip.
Fill in the hole and then drill into the hill.	The insect itch was from a tick.
The fish fin is very thick.	It is difficult to skid uphill.
I still need to visit my kin.	The wig is thin and trim.
Brick and Tin is a restaurant in Israel.	Isabel will win the big-ticket.

Table 4-14e. Vowel: /ɪ/

Context: Sentence Level- Single Occurrence

We have <u>six</u> eggs left.	The <u>fig</u> tree did not bloom.
We can <u>rig</u> up a solution.	We left a small <u>tip</u> for the waitress.
I have a fear of the loud <u>drill</u>.	The cookbook calls for Cheese <u>Whiz</u>.
The goalie <u>kicked</u> the ball hard.	You are skating on <u>thin</u> ice.
What <u>if</u> I lose the password?	I'm having surgery on my <u>hip</u> tomorrow.
You can <u>win</u> the prize for the contest!	You should <u>chill</u> white wine.
I took a <u>pill</u> for my headache.	We <u>still</u> have to do homework.
The water bottle won't <u>spill</u> when turned over.	We need a new oven <u>mitt</u>.
I <u>quit</u> my new job today.	The Good Year <u>blimp</u> got loose.
I fell on the ice and busted my <u>lip</u>.	The shirt has a new <u>rip</u> on the sleeve.
I have a long to-do <u>list</u> now.	The auto shop can <u>fix</u> my car.
Do you know <u>him</u> or not?	The party <u>dip</u> was yummy.
The bug bite really does <u>itch</u>.	The Halloween candy made me <u>sick</u>.
<u>Did</u> they call you too?	Cool <u>Whip</u> makes great desserts.
The doctor gave me a new <u>pill</u>.	I ate a Hershey <u>kiss</u> after lunch.
Amazon can <u>ship</u> the package soon.	I felt <u>ill</u> after the hard exam.
We had a candle-<u>lit</u> meal.	Can you <u>dim</u> the lights for me?
Moles can <u>dig</u> up your whole yard.	Her <u>wig</u> looks perfect!
Dad likes to <u>flip</u> our pancakes onto the plate.	Look <u>in</u> the green bucket first.
Where <u>is</u> the best restaurant?	We had <u>shrimp</u> and bacon for brunch.

Table 4-15a. Vowel: /æ/						
Context: Word Level						
Ab	Cab	Gab	Lab	Tab	Crab	Grab
At	Bat	Cat	Fat	Hat	Mat	Rat
Ad	Chat	Flat	Glad	Had	Bad	Dad
Ask	Crack	Mad	Sad	Cap	Gap	Lap
App	Map	Nap	Tap	Clap	Flap	Snap
Vast	Pack	Sack	Snack	Black	Shack	Track
Tan	Cash	Dash	Mash	Clash	Crash	Flash
Badge	Gal	Pal	Wax	Bath	Match	Math
Back	Jack	Rack	Nats	Pat	Sat	Bag
Tag	Rag	Have	Wag	Laugh	Calf	Class
Grass	Glass	Pass	Lack	Bash	Mask	Past
Blast	Span	Plan	Van	Fan	Can	Ran
Man	Dan	Ban	Lamp	Stamp	Ramp	Damp
Band	Hand	Land	Sand	Brand	Stand	Fast
Last	Task	Smash	Brat	Fad	Catch	Drab

Table 4-15b. Vowel: /æ/		
Context: Phrase Level- Repeated Occurrence		
Back pack	Gal pal	Ran past
Pass class	Cash app	Mad gab
Grab bag	Math lab	Had blast
Nats bat	Catch nap	Can ask
Van ad	Smash hand	Sand crab
Damp rag	Fast track	Drab band
Black cat	Fat man	Glad laugh
Plan ban	Flat map	Grass sap
Glass rack	Brag badge	Lack cab
Have tab	Pat brat	Wax stamp
Dad clash	Bath mat	Had crash
Rat shack	Span fad	Hat flap
Bad cap	Snap flash	Ramp stand
Brand tag	Snack sack	Sad dash
At last	Fan chat	Land gap

Table 4-15c. Vowel: /æ/				
Context: Phrase Level- Single Occurrence				
Ab work	Take cab	Loud gab	Science lab	New tab
Yell at	Bat girl	Cat meow	Fat cow	Felt hat
Read ad	Will chat	Flat bed	Feel glad	Had one
Ask me	Loud crack	Feel mad	Felt sad	Ball cap
Free app	Google map	Need nap	Tap water	Loud clap
Very vast	Pack up	Large sack	Eat snack	Color black
Sun tan	Need cash	Make a dash	Mash up	We clash
Police badge	My gal	New pal	Candle wick	Bubble bath
Be back	Know Jack	Shoe rack	Watch Nats	Pat head
Game of tag	Dirty rag	Have time	Wag tail	Laugh hard
Grass blade	Broken glass	Metro pass	Lack one	Bash in
Loud blast	Wing span	New plan	Blue van	Loud fan
Best man	Call Dan	Phone ban	Bright lamp	Postage stamp
Loud band	My hand	Bought land	White sand	Brand new
Last call	Big task	Smash button	A brat	New fad
Giant crab	Grab one	Old shack	Gym track	Mask up
Yoga mat	Saw rat	Car crash	Big flash	Coke can
Bad news	Call me	Match set	Like math	Skateboard ramp
Wide gap	Run lap	Sat down	Bag groceries	Flower stand
Flap wings	Snap button	Sore calf	Early class	Big catch
Past time	Ran in	Damp floor	Fast lane	Looks drab

Table 4-15d. Vowel: /æ/
Context: Sentence Level- Repeated Occurrence

To get <u>flat</u> <u>abs,</u> you must work <u>fast</u>.

<u>Track</u> <u>shack</u> is <u>having</u> a brand-new sale.

<u>Jack</u> will <u>pass</u> along the <u>badge</u>.

<u>Pat</u> is in <u>math</u> <u>class</u>.

The <u>black</u> <u>cap</u> was under the <u>ramp</u>.

I took a <u>lap</u> around the <u>fast</u> <u>track</u>.

I <u>grabbed</u> my bus <u>pass</u> with the <u>tag</u>.

The <u>van</u> <u>has</u> a <u>flat</u> tire.

<u>Val</u> is my <u>gal</u> <u>pal</u>.

The <u>vast</u> <u>sand</u> <u>clashes</u> with the <u>grass</u>.

The <u>band</u> is playing on the <u>fat</u> <u>stand</u>.

My <u>map</u> <u>app</u> said to take another <u>lap</u>.

Use <u>sand</u> <u>and</u> <u>wax</u> to clean the <u>bathtub</u>.

The phone <u>ban</u> <u>spanned</u> across a long <u>gap</u>.

The <u>laptop</u> in the <u>backpack</u> <u>has</u> a big <u>crack</u>.

<u>Grab</u> a <u>swag</u> <u>bag</u> by the front door.

We will <u>catch</u> a <u>sand</u> <u>crab</u> for dinner.

The <u>man</u> <u>ran</u> in a <u>fast</u> <u>flash</u> around the <u>track</u>.

Use the <u>back</u> <u>scratcher</u> with your left <u>hand</u>.

The <u>bathmat</u> <u>matches</u> the color of <u>grass</u>.

The <u>bad</u> <u>blast</u> was from the <u>last</u> <u>crash</u>.

Run down the <u>damp</u> <u>ramp</u> and <u>land</u> here.

You <u>have</u> to open a new <u>tab</u> with <u>cash</u>.

<u>Jack</u> did <u>ask</u> if I <u>have</u> the <u>cash</u> <u>app</u>.

The <u>mad</u> <u>crab</u> is not on <u>land</u>.

I <u>sat</u> on the <u>mad</u> <u>cat</u> today.

Your <u>snack</u> is in the <u>black</u> <u>sack</u>.

She made a <u>mad</u> <u>dash</u> to the <u>glass</u> chair.

<u>Jack</u> took a <u>nap</u> in the <u>grass</u>.

The <u>last</u> <u>task</u> on the list is to <u>snap</u> your fingers.

This <u>class</u> was a <u>blast</u> from the <u>past</u>.

The <u>fat</u> <u>calf</u> <u>sat</u> in the <u>grass</u>.

The <u>tan</u> <u>van</u> <u>had</u> a <u>scratch</u> <u>that</u> <u>matched</u>.

The <u>last</u> <u>man</u> made a <u>mad</u> <u>dash</u> to the front.

My <u>hand</u> hit the <u>glass</u> off the top <u>rack</u>.

I <u>smashed</u> the <u>bratty</u> <u>gnat</u> with my <u>hand</u>.

<u>Brand</u> names are a <u>drab</u> <u>fad</u>.

The <u>black</u> <u>bat</u> and <u>cat</u> are costume <u>masks</u>.

The <u>lack</u> of <u>snacks</u> made me <u>sad</u>.

<u>Dan</u> <u>can</u> <u>laugh</u> <u>at</u> himself.

Table 4-15e. Vowel: /æ/

Context: Sentence Level- Single Occurrence

The giant <u>crab</u> is looking for food.

I took a <u>cab</u> to the party.

I will <u>grab</u> lunch now.

The <u>task</u> is now to clean up.

The dress is a name <u>brand</u>.

I <u>have</u> to run back home first.

The TA agent lost his <u>badge</u>.

I need a <u>snack</u> before dinner.

The candle <u>wax</u> is on the table.

We <u>sat</u> down for the Uber.

The news often makes me <u>sad</u>.

We will <u>chat</u> with the professor.

What is the <u>plan</u> for Monday?

Trevor Noah makes me <u>laugh</u>!

Did he <u>ask</u> you about the show?

Mind the <u>gap</u> when stepping off the train.

What is your favorite <u>band</u>?

Remember to cut the <u>tags</u> off the shirt.

The tennis <u>match</u> is before 2:00.

There is still one grocery <u>bag</u> in the trunk.

The <u>grass</u> needs to be cut.

The science <u>lab</u> is not open.

I didn't get a <u>suntan</u> this summer.

My shoe <u>rack</u> is quite full.

Will you turn on the <u>lamp</u>?

He is a <u>fast</u> speaker.

Check the <u>map</u> to see if we are lost.

There was a loud <u>clap</u> of thunder.

It occurred in a <u>snap</u>!

We <u>had</u> to call for reservations.

What should I <u>pack</u> for my trip?

They only take <u>cash</u>, not credit cards.

Do you like to run around the <u>track</u>?

I need a <u>stamp</u> for the letter.

Take a picture with the <u>flash</u>.

I <u>lack</u> confidence when public speaking.

I don't think I'll <u>pass</u> the test.

I'd be <u>glad</u> to do this.

I <u>ran</u> around the house looking for my shoe.

I lost the pen <u>cap</u>.

Table 4-16a. Vowel: /ʌ/						
Context: Word Level						
Up	Cup	Suck	Budge	Pulse	Trunk	Blood
Ugh	Bud	Thud	Pup	Struck	Truck	What
Um	But	Puck	Mutt	Hut	Nut	Putt
Us	Shut	Blunt	Just	Must	Front	Trust
Hunt	Thrust	Cuts	Duct	Crush	Crust	Gust
Flush	Crushed	Thrusts	Rust	Bust	Rush	Brushed
Rushed	Brush	Flushed	Blush	Gush	Hush	Gushed
Blushed	Hushed	Shuts	Tuck	Duck	Cups	Stunt
Brunt	Grunt	Rough	Tuft	Nuts	Bunt	Pluck
Luck	Clutch	Puff	Cuff	Huff	Runt	Strut
Love	Cut	Rut	Punch	Hunch	Munch	Lunch
Crunch	Brunch	Such	Touch	Much	Dutch	Mulch
Bunch	Hutch	Lush	Slush	Plush	Mush	Hunts
Stuck	Buck	Snuck	Bulk	Dusk	Dust	Junk
Chunk	Bunk	Shrunk	Husk	Dusts	Stuff	Mud

Table 4-16b. Vowel: /ʌ/		
Context: Phrase Level- Repeated Occurrence		
Suck up	Love brunch	Mud thud
Rough clutch	Junk stuff	Lunch bunch
Duck hunts	Blunt cut	Gust thrusts
Touch cuff	Munch nuts	Ugh um
Much trust	What hunch	Shut hutch
Mulch dust	Blood rush	Struck pulse
Budge trunk	Truck front	Must crunch
Nut Hut	Hushed grunt	Blushed dusk
Dusts bunk	Runt pup	Chunk bulk
Mutt strut	Brunt cuts	Just us
Such luck	Gut punch	Husk tuft
Rushed mush	Brushed crust	Cups gushed
Hush shut	Stuck rut	Dutch stunt
Pluck rust	Gush blush	Crushed hunt
Plush brush	Flushed slush	Tough thrust

Table 4-16c. Vowel: /ʌ/				
Context: Phrase Level- Single Occurrence				
Up high	Red cup	Suck straw	Don't budge	Fast pulse
Oh ugh	Flower bud	Loud thud	Old pup	Struck out
Um no	But why	Hockey puck	Small mutt	Pizza Hut
With us	Shut door	Blunt corner	Just because	Must do
Bear hunt	Thrust engine	Paper cuts	Duct tape	Crush it
Flush fast	Crushed pineapple	Over thrusts	See rust	Huge sculpture
Rushed away	Brush stroke	Feel flushed	Red blush	Big gush
Felt blushed	Hushed dog	Shuts down	Tuck in	Duck down
Bear the brunt	Loud grunt	Rough day	Tuft hair	Nuts and bolts
No luck	Black clutch	Puff Kleenex	Cuff links	Huff Post
Love to read	Paper cut	In a rut	Drink punch	Big hunch
Captain Crunch	Go to brunch	Such as	Touch this	Too much
Grape bunch	Wooden hutch	Lush fields	Snow slush	Plush pillow
Stuck here	Big buck	Snuck out	Bulk sale	Now dusk
Huge chunk	Bunk bed	Has shrunk	Corn husk	Dusts webs
Car trunk	Found blood	Rush hour	Brushed metal	Munch food
New truck	What now	Hush now	She gushed	Dutch pancake
Tree nut	Mini putt	Solo cups	Stunt performer	Eat mush
Front door	Trust me	Bunt ball	Pluck feathers	Less dust
Pizza crust	Gust of wind	Little runt	Strut around	More stuff
Eat lunch	Tree mulch	Hunts deer	Junk food	Dirty mud

Table 4-16d. Vowel: /ʌ/
Context: Sentence Level- Repeated Occurrence

The stuck bunch wouldn't budge.	The paper cut caused a blood rush.
Our lunch bunch meets out front.	The rust flower bud was crushed.
We brushed the crust with butter.	The stunt was like a gut punch.
There was too much mulch dust.	I don't have much trust in us.
The wind gust struck a pulse.	The blunt thud of the mud was heard.
We would love for you to join us for brunch.	This junk stuff feels like a rut.
The blunt cut didn't hurt much.	The truck clutch is a little rough.
You must suck it up and keep going.	The mutt strut is such a fun parade.
For lunch, I munched on nuts.	What is your gut hunch?
Um, can you shut the wooden hutch?	The wind gust thrusts the hutch shut.
The blush did touch your cuff.	The shut trunk won't budge.
The front of the truck was crushed.	The Nut Hut is shut for summer.
We dusted the bunk with a brush.	Hush, there is no such luck.
The hunter was lucky he wasn't cut.	The upset uncle was upstairs.
The ugly duck was stuck in a rut.	We plucked the plush one in a rush.
The ugly mush was an upgrade.	He is done cutting the butter.
The truck got stuck in some mud.	Mom loves us very much.
The lush sun is up in the sky.	There is some water in the mugs and cups.
There were enough floods to shut the town.	Come to London this Sunday for fun.
The nun did nothing but hum in choir.	The country is sunny and young.

Table 4-16e. Vowel: /ʌ/

Context: Sentence Level- Single Occurrence

Put your name on your <u>cup</u>.

You have to <u>trust</u> me.

I bought a new red <u>truck</u>.

We went to Pizza <u>Hut</u> for dinner.

Have you tried Credo <u>blush</u>?

We will have our air <u>ducts</u> cleaned.

My new dog is a <u>mutt</u>.

He <u>rushed</u> himself to the hospital.

She gave <u>us</u> a small gift.

Go <u>up</u> the stairs and turn left.

I <u>love</u> the new ice cream.

Do you want to go to <u>brunch</u>?

My black <u>clutch</u> will match the dress.

The flower <u>bud</u> is starting to bloom.

The <u>duck</u> stays in the pond year-round.

The <u>cups</u> for the party are all gone.

Please do not <u>touch</u> the wallpaper.

Do you like thin or thick pizza <u>crust</u>?

I'm having <u>blood</u> drawn in the morning.

We are meeting for <u>lunch</u> at 2:00.

Please <u>shut</u> the door behind you.

<u>What</u> do you think now?

Put the packages in the <u>trunk</u>.

We <u>must</u> try the new restaurant.

There is <u>rust</u> on the metal chair.

We will wait <u>just</u> for you.

The little <u>pup</u> is adorable!

I'm on the <u>hunt</u> for a good sale.

<u>Um</u>, which way do we go?

I wish you good <u>luck</u>.

This grape <u>bunch</u> is very good.

I still <u>cut</u> out coupons weekly.

I <u>brush</u> my hair every morning.

I <u>tuck</u> my kids into bed at 8:00 every night.

<u>Nuts</u> make a healthy snack.

That is <u>such</u> a lie!

I had a <u>hunch</u> this would happen.

Please use the <u>front</u> door before 6:00.

A big wind <u>gust</u> blew through.

The garden needs new <u>mulch</u>.

Table 4-17a. Vowel: /a/						
Context: Word Level						
Ah	Stop	Sock	Lodge	Romp	God	Not
Got	Hot	Cot	Shot	Spot	Plot	Lot
Scott	Dot	Knot	Slot	Rot	Yacht	Clot
Tot	Trot	Jot	Watt	Blot	Swat	Throng
Swan	Want	Lots	Doll	Law	Dolls	Laws
Drop	Pop	Hop	Top	Bop	Cop	Crop
Mop	Plop	Sop	Lop	Log	Fog	Grog
Hog	Bog	Cog	Locks	Job	Jog	Docks
Honk	Clock	Lock	Dock	Socks	Mocks	Jogs
Prop	Shop	Chop	Flop	Slop	Clop	Hops
Swap	Chops	Props	Swaps	Smock	Tock	Block
Stock	Shock	Doc	Flock	Mock	Frock	Stops
Stocks	Romps	Spots	Plots	Dots	Knots	Slots
Rots	Yachts	Clots	Drops	Mops	Clocks	Tops

Table 4-17b. Vowel: /a/		
Context: Phrase Level- Repeated Occurrence		
Doll socks	Stocks drop	Chop shop
Got mop	Sock hop	Swap prop
Mock smock	Lock dock	Stock drops
Top locks	Yacht docks	God plot
Not lot	Hot trot	Yachts honk
Flop clock	Swap cop	Ah stop
Frock mocks	Lop chops	Mops spots
Block hops	Hog bog	Stops jog
Shock Scott	Crop plots	Blot spot
Want laws	Throng clog	Fog grog
Swaps props	Slop job	Watt knot
Top knots	Swan flock	Tot cot
Log rots	Clocks tock	Dot dots

Table 4-17c. Vowel: /a/				
Context: Phrase Level- Single Occurrence				
Ah what	Stop there	Clean sock	Big lodge	Romp around
Got it	Very hot	Need cot	Took shot	Spot pet
Call Scott	Dot lines	Tie knot	In slot	Root rot
Little tot	Fast trot	Jot down	Power watt	Blot ink
Pretty swan	Want this	Lots more	Baby doll	Know law
Drop mail	Soda pop	Bunny hop	Top shelf	Bop head
Mop floor	Big plop	Sop juice	Lop sided	Wooden log
The hog	Wet bog	A cog	Pick locks	Like job
Car honk	Check clock	Lock door	Dock boat	Wear socks
Prop here	Window shop	Chop up	Flop down	The slop
Swap it	Chops meat	The props	Swaps items	Smock dress
Stock market	Felt shock	Google doc	Sheep flock	Mock me
The stocks	Romps around	See spots	Book plots	Connect dots
Tree rots	Have yachts	Blood clots	Drops here	Mops floor
Oh God	Not now	See cop	Grow crop	Hear tock
Will plot	Parking lot	More fog	Felt grog	Party frock
Have yacht	Blood clot	Go jog	Boat docks	Tie knots
SWAT team	Crowd throng	Mocks me	She jogs	Wooden clocks
Collect dolls	Strict laws	Clop loudly	Hops away	Block play

Table 4-17d. Vowel: /a/

Context: Sentence Level- Repeated Occurrence

Mom smocked socks for the doll.	The stocks dropped after the laws changed.
Scott and Laura went to the sock hop.	The yacht went to a chop shop.
Let's swap the props with the clock.	There are not a lot of swans in the flock.
The top job was very sloppy.	The cops shocked Scott with a traffic violation.
The tot is on the cot with purple dots.	Mom makes mock frocks for dolls.
The clock flopped on the top shelf.	Blot the ink spot with the mop.
The roadblock made me stop my jog.	The rotten log is in the bog.
Ah, we should stop because of fog.	The plots in the bog are for crops.
The throng of people clogged the blockade.	The fog in the bog made me groggy.
Yachts are measured in knots, not watts.	I want to play dot to dots.
Wipe the top spots with the mops.	We want to swap the laws.
It's her job to swap out the props.	They chopped the lock off the dock.

Table 4-17e. Vowel: /a/
Context: Sentence Level- Single Occurrence

Where is your bus <u>stop</u>?	I need new <u>socks</u> now.
Did you get the new <u>job</u>?	Hearing the news <u>shocked</u> me.
<u>Tots</u> to Teens is a clothing store.	Did you meet <u>Scott</u> at the reunion?
The door will <u>lock</u> behind you.	Use the bread to <u>sop</u> up the oil.
The <u>yachts</u> at Navy Yard are big.	Something just <u>plopped</u> in the water.
I <u>dropped</u> my keys through the grate.	The beautiful <u>swan</u> is in the lake.
The horses <u>trot</u> down this trail.	Put a <u>dot</u> next to the ones you don't need.
Is it <u>hot</u> or cold outside?	The <u>lodge</u> has a fireplace and restaurant.
We do <u>not</u> have time for that.	We had a <u>lot</u> of food for Thanksgiving.
<u>Jot</u> this down quickly before you forget.	I <u>want</u> to try the new workout class.
Have you been to the <u>top</u> of the Monument?	It's stuck in the mail <u>slot</u>.
It was a good <u>shot</u>.	I am looking for a parking <u>spot</u>.
There are more traffic <u>stops</u> now.	Please don't <u>block</u> the road.
These are the time <u>slots</u> available.	My car is now in the <u>shop</u>.
The <u>clock</u> in the room is broken.	The tired cat <u>flopped</u> down near the bed.
He <u>mocks</u> them for their work.	I always <u>jog</u> in the morning.
The <u>fog</u> is very bad today.	What <u>crop</u> is growing in the field?
Do you know how <u>laws</u> are made?	There was a <u>throng</u> of people at the show.
The <u>plot</u> of the book is very good.	The <u>SWAT</u> team is outside of the building.
The skis are <u>propping</u> up the door.	The big <u>log</u> rolled into the creek.

Table 4-18a. Vowel: /ɔ/						
Context: Word Level						
Aw	Cloth	Cough	Broth	Bought	Cross	Long
Ought	Thought	Moth	Froth	Sloth	Mall	Call
All	Moths	Sloths	Cloths	Paul	Cause	Loss
Fall	Saul	Hawk	Gall	Ball	Hall	Wall
Tall	Y'all	Brought	Caught	Pause	Gauze	Fought
Gloss	Floss	Halls	Walls	Lost	Malls	Calls
Clause	Dawn	Pawn	Gone	Drawn	Lawn	Mauve
Caulk	Squawk	Walk	Jaw	Paw	Boss	Raw
Haul	Gnaw	Moss	Walks	Jaws	Paws	Hauls
Strong	Wrong	Ross	Song	Dog	Broad	Lawn
Spawn	Shawn	Fawn	Hawks	Yawn	Balls	Haunt

Table 4-18b. Vowel: /ɔ/		
Context: Phrase Level- Repeated Occurrence		
Long song	Call Ross	Fall ball
Bought cloth	Dog paw	Mauve wall
Hawk squawk	Gnaw paws	Caught pawn
Gone wrong	Mall hall	Strong pause
Sloth jaw	Broad halls	Boss calls
Broth froth	Tall cross	All gloss
Lost cause	Fought loss	Dawn drawn
Moth balls	Lawn fawn	Lawn moss

Table 4-18c. Vowel: /ɔ/				
Context: Phrase Level- Single Occurrence				
Aw cute	Terry cloth	Cough loud	Chicken broth	Bought this
Ought to	I thought	Luna moth	Coffee froth	Slow sloth
All done	Found moths	Slow sloths	Cleaning cloths	Meet Paul
Fall down	Know Saul	See hawk	The gall	Throw ball
Tall guy	Hi y'all	Brought home	Caught fish	Pause it
Shiny gloss	Dental floss	The halls	Big walls	Lost dog
Santa Clause	New dawn	Chess pawn	Written clause	Drawn out
Caulk tub	Loud squawk	Walk away	Little jaw	Cat paw
Haul boxes	Gnaw at me	Moss rock	Take walks	Jaws movie
Strong arm	Wrong one	Know Ross	Like song	New dog
Did spawn	Meet Shawn	Young fawn	Seattle Hawks	Big yawn
Don't cross	Long throw	Shopping malls	Calls home	Throw balls
Big mall	Call me	Pretty lawn	Color mauve	Old haunt
Cause that	Big loss	Big boss	Raw dough	Need gauze
The hall	Red wall	Bear paws	Truck hauls	Fought off

Table 4-18d. Vowel: /ɔ/
Context: Sentence Level- Repeated Occurrence

I'll <u>call</u> <u>Ross</u> about <u>fall</u> <u>ball</u>.

They painted the <u>long</u> <u>halls</u> <u>mauve</u>.

The <u>long</u> <u>pause</u> meant it had <u>gone</u> <u>wrong</u>.

Don't <u>cross</u> your <u>boss</u>, <u>Paul</u>.

The cute <u>froth</u> is a <u>lost</u> <u>cause</u>.

There is a cute <u>fawn</u> on the <u>lawn</u> in the <u>moss</u>.

I <u>lost</u> in chess because my <u>pawn</u> was <u>caught</u>.

I <u>thought</u> the <u>song</u> was very <u>long</u>.

<u>Y'all</u> are <u>all</u> very <u>tall</u>.

It's a <u>long</u> <u>haul</u> with the <u>dog</u>.

The <u>moth</u> <u>balls</u> <u>gnawed</u> through the <u>cloth</u>.

Better <u>Call</u> <u>Saul</u> is a <u>long</u> series.

The loud <u>hawk</u> <u>squawk</u> scared the <u>fawn</u>.

The <u>dog</u> <u>caught</u> his <u>paw</u> on the <u>wall</u>.

We like to <u>walk</u> the <u>halls</u> of the <u>mall</u>.

The <u>hawk</u> and <u>sloth</u> <u>jaws</u> are very <u>strong</u>.

The <u>cloth</u> has lots of <u>moth</u> <u>balls</u>.

The shiny <u>mauve</u> car is <u>all</u> <u>gloss</u>.

My <u>boss</u> <u>called</u> me to give a <u>strong</u> lecture.

We <u>bought</u> the chicken <u>broth</u> to <u>froth</u>.

<u>Aww</u>, I <u>ought</u> to <u>call</u> <u>Paul</u> and thank him.

This <u>fall</u>, we will play <u>ball</u> on the <u>lawn</u>.

Use the <u>cloth</u>, so you don't <u>cough</u> on <u>Shawn</u>.

<u>Ross</u> will <u>haunt</u> you until it's <u>brought</u> back.

I <u>thought</u> the <u>moths</u> had <u>jaws</u>.

We <u>walked</u> the <u>halls</u> at <u>dawn</u>.

Table 4-18e. Vowel: /ɔ/	
Context: Sentence Level- Single Occurrence	
Do you like the Seattle <u>Seahawks</u>?	Add chicken <u>broth</u> to the soup.
I <u>bought</u> this at the store.	Don't <u>cross</u> the double yellow line.
He threw a <u>long</u> pass down the field.	The <u>froth</u> is a heart shape.
Each morning, I move at a <u>sloth's</u> pace.	There is a big <u>mall</u> in Minnesota.
<u>Call</u> me before you leave work.	These <u>cloths</u> are for cleaning.
The team had a big <u>loss</u> on Saturday.	Do they know what <u>caused</u> it?
He had the <u>gall</u> to do what?	We <u>caught</u> a fish in the Potomac.
Did you meet <u>Paul</u> at the reunion?	The formal <u>ball</u> is tonight.
Take a left at the end of the <u>hall</u>.	We are painting one accent <u>wall</u> red.
Can you <u>pause</u> the movie?	I need <u>gauze</u> and a band-aid.
Mary <u>lost</u> her dog over the weekend.	The shopping <u>malls</u> are closing.
She <u>calls</u> home every Friday night.	This place is my old <u>haunt</u>.
I love the color <u>mauve</u>.	I did eat the <u>raw</u> cookie dough.
She is my big <u>boss</u> on campus.	This is my favorite <u>song</u>!
I take at least two <u>walks</u> every day.	We wondered where you had <u>gone</u>.
These are big <u>walls</u> for the room.	You have a beautiful <u>lawn</u>.
They <u>fought</u> over which route to take.	I have TMJ, so my <u>jaw</u> often hurts.
My cat swipes his <u>paw</u> under the door.	You need a U-<u>Haul</u> for this stuff.
That is a <u>broad</u> way of thinking.	A <u>yawn</u> can be contagious.
I'm being monitored like a <u>hawk</u>.	It was <u>drawn</u> out on a map.

Table 4-19a. Vowel: /ʊ/						
Context: Word Level						
Put	Look	Foot	Bush	Full	Good	Wolf
Cook	Crook	Book	Took	Shook	Hoof	Hook
Brook	Nook	Rook	Looked	Booked	Books	Cooked
Hooked	Wood	Stood	Pull	Would	Woof	Push
Soot	Wool	Butch	Could	Should	Bull	Hood

Table 4-19b. Vowel: /ʊ/				
Context: Phrase Level- Repeated Occurrence				
Look good	Cook book	Full bush	Would should	Looked butch
Could pull	Put hook	Wolf hoof	Bull wool	Took rook
Shook foot	Nook crook	Cooked wood	Brook soot	Push pull

Table 4-19c. Vowel: /ʊ/				
Context: Phrase Level- Single Occurrence				
Put here	Look down	Hurt foot	Hooked fish	Fire soot
Cook dinner	The crook	Read book	Wood barrel	Itchy wool
Streaming brook	Little nook	Rook card	Stood up	Looks nice
Green bush	Full basket	Good enough	Gray wolf	Could you
Took one	Shook up	Horse hoof	The hook	Should we
Looked up	Booked room	Read books	Cooked lunch	Running bull
Pull down	Would you	Hear woof	Push hard	Car hood

Table 4-19d. Vowel: /ʊ/	
Context: Sentence Level- Repeated Occurrence	
The <u>book</u> <u>nook</u> <u>looks</u> <u>good</u>.	The <u>cookbook</u> is <u>full</u> of <u>good</u> recipes.
<u>Put</u> the <u>fishhook</u> in the <u>brook</u>.	We <u>cooked</u> the <u>butcher's</u> meat over <u>wood</u>.
The <u>cook</u> <u>overlooked</u> the <u>wood</u> stove.	<u>Put</u> <u>good</u> filters on your <u>Facebook</u> page.
The <u>crook</u> found the <u>book</u> in the <u>nook</u>.	I like pizza <u>cooked</u> over <u>wood</u> without <u>soot</u>.
The <u>bull</u> and <u>woof</u> <u>stood</u> in the grass.	Don't think about <u>would've</u>, <u>should've</u>, <u>could've</u>.
I have a <u>bull</u> <u>wool</u> sock on my <u>foot</u>.	The <u>crook</u> <u>took</u> the <u>rook</u> from the chessboard.
<u>Push</u> the <u>hook</u> up and then <u>pull</u> the door open.	I <u>shook</u> my <u>foot</u> when it got wet in the <u>brook</u>.

Table 4-19e. Vowel: /ʊ/	
Context: Sentence Level- Single Occurrence	
Are you on <u>Facebook</u>?	What is your favorite <u>book</u>?
What does it <u>look</u> like?	Was it <u>good</u> or bad?
<u>Would</u> you want to grab lunch?	<u>Could</u> you email me that information?
I really don't like to <u>cook</u>.	The <u>wolf</u> howled at the moon.
We had to <u>push</u> the car out of the road.	Please <u>pull</u> into lane one.
The wreck <u>shook</u> me up.	There is a <u>crook</u> in the area.
Don't beat around the <u>bush</u>.	I am still <u>full</u> from lunch.
He's like a <u>bull</u> in a china shop.	I <u>should</u> have made a reservation for us.
<u>Put</u> the dirty dishes in the sink.	We have a <u>hook</u> for the coats.
The horse <u>hoof</u> needs new shoes.	I hit my <u>foot</u> on the table leg.
I <u>cooked</u> dinner for my roommate.	They have a <u>wood</u>-fired pizza oven.
The condo has a cute little <u>nook</u>.	He <u>looked</u> at me for confirmation.
The <u>butcher</u> at the deli is great.	I <u>took</u> the bus to work.
The <u>rook</u> is a chess piece.	I have a new <u>wool</u> coat for winter!
The streaming <u>brook</u> is freezing cold.	The <u>soot</u> from the fireplace is everywhere.

Table 4-20a. Vowel: /u/					
Context: Word Level					
Ew	Goose	Loose	Loop	Shoot	Loot	Tomb
Oops	Tube	Food	Mood	Rude	Roof	Cool
Ooze	Pool	Rule	Stool	Tool	Boom	Noon
Use	Room	Zoom	Moon	Soon	Hoop	Soup
Moose	Boot	Root	Cruise	Whose	Who	Lose
News	Stews	Juice	Bruce	Bruise	Prune	Seuss
Sleuth	Snooze	Spruce	Truce	Woo	Zeus	Boo
Zoo	Fool	Move	Hoot	Suit	Coop	Poof
Doom	Goof	Two	You	Do	Hue	Clue
Too	Group	Dupe	True	Fruit	Route	Youth
Truth	Proof	Boost	Duke	Booth	Flute	Roost
Chute	Scoop	Stoop	Luke	Spook	Droop	Choose
Shoes	Cue	Blue	To	Crew	Screw	Fuse
Due	Muse	Ewe	Rue	Sue	Glue	Flu
Chew	View	Through	Drew	Troop	Threw	Fuel

Table 4-20b. Vowel: /u/		
Context: Phrase Level- Repeated Occurrence		
Shoot hoop	Sleuth clue	Moose zoo
Oops goof	Cruise crew	Lose proof
Too soon	Cool tomb	Dupe fool
Use snooze	Stews food	Zoom rule
Noon boost	Prune juice	Chew fruit
Rude Duke	Spook Luke	Youth group
Pool room	Ew ooze	Boot shoes
Blue moon	Scoop soup	Move stool
Two ewes	Stoop droop	Lose suit
Through chute	To Sue	True truth
You do	Choose booth	Roof tool
Who's who	Loose screw	Spruce root
Threw glue	News doom	Woo Zeus
Goose hoot	Due truce	View route
Cue Bruce	Fuel tube	Mood hue

Table 4-20c. Vowel: /u/				
Context: Phrase Level- Single Occurrence				
Ew gross	See goose	Loose nail	Loop up	Oh shoot
Oh oops	Tube cap	Get food	Bad mood	Was rude
Ooze out	Swimming pool	Follow rule	Wooden stool	Tool kit
Use pen	Quiet room	Zoom call	Full moon	Very soon
Brown moose	Boot print	Flower root	Take cruise	Whose turn
Watch news	Make stews	Orange juice	Know Bruce	Have bruise
The sleuth	Snooze button	Spruce up	Call truce	Oh woo
National Zoo	Big fool	Move on	Hoot owl	Nice suit
Doom day	Goof off	Two people	You know	Do this
Too much	Group work	Dupe me	Was true	Yummy fruit
Tell truth	Show proof	Boost up	Duke football	Phone booth
Trash chute	Scoop ice cream	Porch stoop	Call Luke	Big spook
Red shoes	Give cue	Blue blouse	To me	Sailing crew
Book due	The muse	Four ewes	Rue day	Know Sue
Chew breakfast	Nice view	Follow through	Drew art	Scout troop
The loot	Large tomb	Eat prune	Dr. Seuss	Play flute
Old roof	Feel cool	Zeus God	Say boo	Ceiling droop
Heard boom	At noon	Chicken coop	Poof be gone	Screw in
Basketball hoop	Tomato soup	Bright hue	Give clue	Glue paper
Who is	Lose weight	This route	The youth	Threw away
Chicken roost	Choose one	Blow a fuse	Have flu	Car fuel

Table 4-20d. Vowel: /u/
Context: Sentence Level- Repeated Occurrence

The goo oozed all over the stoop.

The dues are due for the scout troop.

Bruce needs to be excused from school.

The prune soup at Duke's Grocery is good.

We will salute our troops at the huge ceremony.

Judy introduced me to the new sleuth.

The roof has two loose screws.

Luke blew a fuse in the big room.

Pandas do eat bamboo shoots.

The new rooster flew the coop.

The group needed a boost, so they hit snooze.

The moose and kangaroos are in the zoo.

If you reuse bags, you reduce waste.

Do you like prune juice?

You do know Sue was rude?

My blue boots and shoes are used.

Do you have proof of who is who?

You two should take this route too.

Can you scoop the soup in the blue bowl?

Our Zoom rule is to tell the truth!

Who knew the trail made a loop?

Do moose eat spruce juice?

The fruit produce can be reduced.

The youth group meets on the blue roof.

Put a scoop of food on the stoop of the coop.

The news views can confuse you.

The full moon has blue hues.

The roots of the spruce are near the stoop.

The proof cannot dispute the truth.

The cruise crew can choose their shoes.

June has a big black and blue bruise.

The goose stew is chewy.

Bruce and Drew called a truce.

Luke went to shoot hoops at noon.

Do you chew your fruit?

Can we move two stools?

We threw the glue in the trash chute.

The loud goose hoot spooked me.

The rude Duke is in the pool room.

The loose tube has fuel for the cruise.

Table 4-20e. Vowel: /u/
Context: Sentence Level- Single Occurrence

Can we play duck duck <u>goose</u>?

Have we visited the National <u>Zoo</u> yet?

Sheryl did <u>lose</u> more weight.

The ceiling <u>droops</u> in the middle.

Alex and I are taking a long <u>cruise</u> in May!

I bought a nice <u>suit</u> for my job.

I played the <u>flute</u> in college.

The basketball <u>hoop</u> is in the park.

The show will start at <u>noon</u>.

Scout <u>troop</u> 305 meets upstairs.

I had the <u>flu</u> last year.

The <u>news</u> starts at 6:00 and 7:00.

Will they follow <u>through</u> with the plan?

My dog <u>chewed</u> on my belt.

Is <u>Zeus</u> a Greek or Roman God?

The shade feels very <u>cool</u>.

<u>Who</u> will pick her up from work?

The chicken <u>coop</u> needs more wire.

Should we just call a <u>truce</u>?

The red <u>stool</u> was just painted.

There is a full <u>moon</u> this evening.

I must show <u>proof</u> with my ID.

Dr. <u>Suess</u> is one of my favorite authors.

The hotel waitress was very <u>rude</u>.

Amani is enrolling in <u>Duke</u> this fall.

Is that a real phone <u>booth</u>?

What is in your <u>tool</u> kit?

Karl was in a bad <u>mood</u> this morning.

We had tomato <u>soup</u> with grilled cheese.

I need <u>glue</u>, pen, and paper for the project.

Look for a <u>clue</u> and solve the mystery.

The orange <u>juice</u> is in aisle 4.

King Tut is in a large <u>tomb</u>.

<u>Do</u> this first, not that.

The cannon <u>boom</u> was very loud.

The house has a very old <u>roof</u>.

The <u>prunes</u> are on sale at Shoppers.

The <u>fruit</u> is beside the vegetables.

I don't know where <u>Bruce</u> lives.

Did he <u>choose</u> this one?

Table 4-21a. Vowel: /ɔɪ/						
Context: Word Level						
Oy	Toy	Roy	Coy	Coil	Joy	Poi
Oil	Soy	Boy	Troy	Ploy	Toil	Coin
Oink	Foil	Boil	Soil	Join	Joint	Loin
Oiled	Koi	Void	Hoist	Joist	Moist	Choice
Voice	Noise	Cloy	Boys	Joyce	Point	Joins
Joints	Points	Voids	Hoists	Toys	Coils	Joys
Oils	Oinks	Foils	Boils	Soils	Royce	Foy
Hoy	Ploys	Toils	Roil	Loins	Joists	Voiced
Cloyed	Ployed	Coiled	Oiled	Toiled	Foiled	Boiled
Soiled	Joined	Foist	Foists	Broil	Poise	Floyd
Broiled	Poised	Floyd's	Broiled	Lloyd	Troy's	Spoil
Lloyd's	Spoiled	Roiled	Croix	Spoils	Boyd	Foys
Roils	Choy	Coin	Voile	Joyful	Deploy	Voices
Enjoyed	Voided	Detroit	Employ	Enjoy	Avoid	Employed
Oiler	Oyster	Choices	Hoisted	Poison	Toilet	Royal

Table 4-21b. Vowel: /ɔɪ/				
Context: Phrase Level- Repeated Occurrence				
Spoiled Bok choy	Floyd's oil	Annoy Roy	Joint ploy	Toiled foists
Destroy toy	Oink noise	Oyster oils	Void foist	Oiled joints
Toils foils	Voided Floyd	Alloy foil	Oiled moist	Hoists croix
Soy koi	Coy boy	Employ Troy	Boyd boils	Spoil foy
Coiled joist	Join Joyce	Avoid poison	Employed joyful	Voids coin
Enjoy toys	Poised royal	Voice hoy	Coil toil	Deploy Lloyd
Boys cloy	Hoist joists	Royce coils	Oy joy	Joined ployed
Point choice	Detroit oiler	Decoy choices	Boil soil	Broiled soiled
Poise foiled	Boiled poi	Voiced joys	Enjoyed Lloyd's	Joins ploys

Table 4-21c. Vowel: /ɔɪ/				
Context: Phrase Level- Single Occurrence				
Oy vey	New toy	Call Roy	Coy smile	Coil rope
Oil car	New Soybeans	Oh boy	Know Troy	A ploy
Pig oink	Use foil	Boil water	Need soil	Join hands
Oiled machine	Koi fish	Was void	Hoist up	A joist
My voice	Loud noise	To cloy	The boys	Saw Joyce
Burger joints	More points	Voids it	Hoists up	New toys
Essential oils	More oinks	Foils plan	Boils water	It soils
Hoy look	The ploys	The toils	Winds roil	Pork loins
That cloyed	Was ployed	Coiled up	Oiled up	Toiled away
Soiled shirt	Joined forces	Foist on	Foists goods	Broil dinner
Broiled fish	Was poised	Floyd's house	Broiled heat	Call Lloyd
Lloyd's job	Spoiled food	Felt roiled	Two croix	Spoils kids
Feel joy	Eat poi	Coils up	Voile curtain	Joyful feeling
We toil	A coin	Rolls Royce	Employ people	Enjoy time
Wooden joint	Pork loin	Joists are	Hoisted up	Rat poison
Felt moist	One choice	Foiled plans	The joys	Voiced concern
Point out	Joins forces	Poise balance	Foy feast	Boiled water
Know Floyd	Troy's house	Will spoil	See Boyd	Foys feasts
Deploy military	Hear voices	Avoid mistakes	Was employed	Royal family

Table 4-21d. Vowel: /ɔɪ/
Context: Sentence Level- Repeated Occurrence

The <u>boy</u> has <u>corduroy</u> <u>voile</u> pants.

The <u>boys</u> <u>destroyed</u> their new <u>toys</u>.

We <u>enjoyed</u> our <u>joyful</u> <u>voyage</u>.

The <u>voile</u> curtains are <u>moist</u> and <u>soiled</u>.

You need a <u>coin</u> to use the <u>noisy</u> <u>toilet</u>.

You should <u>coil</u> the <u>doily</u> with the <u>foil</u>.

Can you <u>pinpoint</u> the <u>foiled cloy</u>?

If the <u>soil</u> is <u>moist</u>, there is <u>moisture</u>.

I <u>enjoyed</u> the <u>broiled</u> <u>oysters</u>.

The <u>noisy</u> <u>employees</u> are <u>foiling</u> the <u>ploy</u>.

Keep the Bok <u>choy</u> <u>moist</u> in <u>foil</u>.

The <u>loyal</u> <u>royal</u> <u>enjoys</u> his work.

<u>Boyd</u> can <u>void</u> the <u>oil</u> charge.

You can <u>point</u> to your <u>choice</u> and <u>rejoice</u>.

<u>Detroit</u> is <u>poised</u> for <u>oil</u> sales.

The <u>Croix</u> in the <u>cloisters</u> were <u>hoisted</u> up.

The <u>boiled</u> <u>poi</u> has <u>soybeans</u>.

The <u>oyster</u> <u>oil</u> will keep it <u>moist</u>.

The <u>cowboy</u> at the <u>toyshop</u> is <u>Boyd</u>.

The <u>Royal</u> Family will <u>join</u> their <u>ploys</u>.

<u>Floyd</u> <u>enjoyed</u> his <u>oysters</u> for lunch.

The <u>cowboy</u> was <u>annoyed</u> by the <u>decoy</u>.

<u>Lloyd</u> and <u>Boyd</u> are <u>hoisting</u> the beams.

I <u>avoided</u> the <u>spoiled</u> bok <u>choy</u>.

You can <u>boil</u> or <u>broil</u> the pork <u>loins</u>.

<u>Hoist</u> the <u>joints</u> until they <u>join</u>.

Put <u>ointment</u> on the <u>point</u> of <u>poison</u>.

Is an <u>oink</u> <u>voiced</u> or <u>voiceless</u>?

Did you <u>join</u> the <u>coin</u> or <u>voice</u> club?

It's a <u>choice</u> to <u>avoid</u> the <u>roiling</u> wind.

The <u>employee</u> was <u>annoyed</u> by the <u>boy</u>.

<u>Lloyd</u>, the <u>busboy</u>, <u>enjoys</u> his work.

We had <u>soy</u> and <u>poi</u> near the <u>koi</u> pond.

<u>Hoy</u>, <u>Royce</u> yelled from the <u>oil</u> rig.

<u>Lloyd's</u> <u>toils</u> and <u>foils</u> are small.

<u>Floyd</u> is in the <u>boiler</u> room fixing a <u>coil</u>.

I <u>voiced</u> my <u>joys</u> to the <u>employee</u>.

<u>Joyce</u> <u>cloyed</u> the busy <u>decoys</u>.

<u>Royce</u> is a <u>loyal</u> <u>busboy</u>.

The <u>voiceless</u> need a <u>pointed</u> <u>voice</u>.

Table 4-21e. Vowel: /ɔɪ/

Context: Sentence Level- Single Occurrence

Hoy, I see the big ship!

My appointment is at noon.

We work as a joint team.

The rat poison isn't working.

Please point me in the right direction.

We will rejoice in the morning.

Do you know how to broil dinner?

The cake is soft and moist.

The pig gave a loud oink.

The car needs an oil change.

Our plans were foiled by them.

The boys are playing outside.

I lost my voice when I had the flu.

The milk will spoil if left out.

The furnace needs a new coil.

I found a coin on heads.

This is my grandma's doily.

The workers will hoist up the beam.

You can avoid traffic by walking.

The Royal Family is not home.

It was a joy meeting her.

Vegetarians should eat more soy.

The scarecrow is a decoy.

The band is very noisy.

The students will try to annoy you.

It was a ploy to get money.

We had bok choy for dinner.

The koi pond is beautiful.

Roy said he will work until 7:00.

I love fried oysters in Baton Rouge.

My first choice didn't work out.

They will void the transaction fee.

I hope you enjoy your trip.

Have you been to Hawaii and tried poi?

We joined forces with the students.

A foy is a farewell feast.

Have you read Toil and Trouble?

I am from Detroit, Michigan.

She drives a Rolls Royce!

We are poised for an easy win.

Table 4-22a. Vowel: /aɪ/						
Context: Word Level						
I	Lice	High	Sigh	Thigh	Bright	Flight
I'm	Fright	Knight	Plight	Write	Slight	Mite
Ice	Site	Vice	Wild	Lied	Pride	Fly
I've	Pry	Dry	Try	Fry	Dried	Tried
I'll	Fried	Ride	Cried	Tyke	Tide	Wide
Bye	Cry	Night	Guy	Fight	Might	Hi
Lie	My	Pie	Tie	Why	Bike	Tribe
Hike	Time	Like	Dime	Lime	Rhyme	Pipe
Ripe	Mice	Nice	Rice	Bite	Kite	Height
Light	Right	Sight	Tight	White	Dive	Hive
Live	Eye	Rise	Size	Lies	Wise	Aisle
Tied	Dice	Slice	Thrice	Knives	Twice	Spice
Price	Splice	Bryce	Heist	Buy	Rye	Sky
Skype	Trite	Life	Wife	Strife	Gripe	Stripe
Hype	Wipe	Pike	Glide	Fine	Dine	Line

Table 4-22b. Vowel: /aɪ/		
Context: Phrase Level- Repeated Occurrence		
White ice	I've tried	My height
Dry eyes	Line stripe	Hi, Bryce
Sky rise	Bike ride	Knife fight
High price	Tight time	I lied
Spice aisle	Wise guy	I'll cry
Fried pies	Fly kite	Light hike
Ripe lime	Nice size	Fry rice
Life strife	Wild hive	Slight pride
Mice bite	Fine dine	Dried pipe
Bright night	Live heist	Write rhyme
Why try	Wide tide	Thrice twice
Slice splice	Trite wife	Skype hype
Right side	Like rye	Tie dyed
Sight dime	Buy dice	Site fright
Might gripe	Glide tribe	Wipe vice

		Table 4-22c. Vowel: /aɪ/		
		Context: Phrase Level- Single Occurrence		
I have	See lice	High knees	Big sigh	Chicken thigh
I'm waiting	Stage fright	Knight in armor	The plight	Write down
The ice	New site	The vice	Wild things	He lied
I've known	Don't pry	Dry out	Try now	French fry
I'll be there	Fried dough	Ride bus	He cried	Little tyke
Bye for now	Cry baby	At night	This guy	Huge fight
Tell a lie	My turn	Apple pie	Tie shoe	Why not
Hike up	Is time	Don't like	Found dime	Key lime
Ripe banana	Field mice	Look nice	Cook rice	Big bite
The light	Turn right	Lost sight	Too tight	Black and white
Was live	Blue eye	All rise	One size	Little lies
Tied up	Roll dice	Slice bread	Was thrice	Steak knives
New price	Will splice	Know Bryce	A heist	Buy one
Skype me	Sound trite	Charmed life	His wife	The strife
The hype	Wipe down	Pike's Peak	Can glide	Feel fine
Bright star	Took flight	Might not	Hi there	Wise men
Slight turn	Dust mite	Bike helmet	New tribe	Called twice
Have pride	House fly	Say rhyme	Water pipe	Rye bread
Dried out	Tried to	Kite festival	His height	Don't gripe
Low tide	Wide brim	Dive team	Busy beehive	Dine in
Grocery aisle	Sugar and spice	Blue sky	Zebra stripe	Get in line

Table 4-22d. Vowel: /aɪ/
Context: Sentence Level- Repeated Occurrence

I have a chicken thigh and cherry pie left.

The dried lime makes a nice spice.

I've seen lice and mites here.

I paid a high price for the hike.

It is fine to dine at night.

We are live on Skype this time.

I will buy a light bulb for a dime.

The tie-dyed shirt made me cry.

My eye has a gray stripe.

I thought twice about sky diving.

The fry guy also makes rye bread.

Bryce can tell wise lies.

The rope tied to the dock was spliced twice.

I said hi and bye to my cousin before he left.

The wipe left a line and a stripe.

The pipe looks nice but is spliced thrice.

We went for a night ride on our bikes.

Key lime pie is my favorite kind.

The white knives are slightly dull.

There is a line in the spice aisle.

Bryce said goodbye before his flight.

The high dive is too wide.

The pipe is thrice the size.

He fried rice in record time for dinner.

There was a kite heist last night.

Why was the bike ride so difficult?

He griped when prying off the fried dough.

The ripe lime is white.

The little tyke put up a fight before bedtime.

My right eye is itching.

Why is there ice in the sky tonight?

The limes and rye are in aisle nine.

His wife will buy the dried fruit.

The hive tribe gave a high five.

I might try to write a rhyme.

Bryce will thrive with his tribe.

Your time is a high price to pay.

I tried the high dive twice.

The size of the hype reached far and wide.

The tight end might tie the football game.

Table 4-22e. Vowel: /aɪ/	
Context: Sentence Level- Single Occurrence	
He let out a big <u>sigh</u>	Do you want a chicken <u>thigh</u> or wing?
Look for the <u>bright</u> star.	The big plane took <u>flight</u>.
<u>I</u> am going to the store now.	<u>Why</u> did you go to the beach?
The <u>CIA</u> office is next door.	Do you want <u>rice</u> with your soup?
The <u>dime</u> was on tails.	We have cherry <u>pie</u> for dessert.
It's a roll of the <u>dice</u>.	Add more <u>spice</u> to the casserole.
Check <u>aisle</u> three for more.	She had a <u>bite</u> of cheesecake.
The <u>white</u> sheets are flannel.	The <u>kite</u> festival is this Saturday.
<u>Dive</u> practice is after school today.	John is a <u>wise</u> old man.
He called the office <u>twice</u>.	The <u>sky</u> quickly became cloudy.
What did you <u>buy</u> at the store?	Monday will be just <u>fine</u>!
The green <u>bike</u> is Michelle's.	Do four and store <u>rhyme</u>?
Saturday will be perfect for a <u>hike</u>.	The big <u>fight</u> is at 8:00.
Did you order <u>fried</u> chicken?	Add <u>lime</u> to the ceviche.
Alex <u>might</u> eat the leftovers later.	His <u>pride</u> was definitely impacted.
Do you need <u>ice</u> in your water?	We must say <u>goodbye</u> now.
Don't <u>cry</u> over spilled milk.	What <u>time</u> does the class start?
Are the bananas overly <u>ripe</u>?	<u>Life</u> is full of the unexpected!
The <u>sliced</u> bread is ready to toast.	The <u>sunrise</u> was beautiful today.
<u>Wipe</u> your feet at the front door.	Do you prefer Zoom or <u>Skype</u>?

Table 4-23a. Vocalic /ɹ/					
Context: Word Level					
ER	**AR**	**IRE**	**AIR**	**EAR**	**OR**
Were	Star	Fire	Air	Fear	Born
First	Far	Plier	Where	Year	Short
Skirt	Bark	Tire	Married	Hero	Tore
Herd	Harp	Flier	Square	Hear	Bore
Turn	Art	Ireland	Share	Near	For
Learn	Car	Hire	Dare	Pier	More
Never	Start	Wire	Care	Hearing	Board
Spider	Arm	Admire	Fair	Cheer	Sport
Butter	Guard	Choir	Cherry	Gear	Corn
Hurt	Garlic	Iron	Dairy	Souvenir	Storm
Dirt	Heart	Empire	Hair	Cashier	Morning
Girl	Farm	Tired	Parrot	Cereal	Store
Teacher	Dark	Umpire	Marathon	Weird	North
Dinner	Yard	Liar	Carried	Deer	Fort

Table 4-80. Vocalic /ɹ/				
Context: Phrase Level- Repeated Occurrence				
First born	Turn here	Never hurt	Star hire	Far bark
Ireland souvenir	Start car	Hearing cheer	Bored chores	Orange port
North shore	Umpire liar	Weird sport	Hurt arm	Hear fear
More cereal	Yard dirt	Admire choir	Hear harp	Dairy fair
For marathon	Learn art	Were married	Tore board	Spider herd
Cherry farm	Morning storm	Short year	Dare care	Parrot skirt
Garlic butter	Deer fort	Store cashier	Tired teacher	Girl hero
Carried gear	Near pier	Air tire	Wire plier	Four square
Share flier	Dinner corn	Dark hair	Guard empire	Iron fire

Table 4-23b. Vocalic /ɹ/				
Context: Phrase Level- Single Occurrence				
Airtight box	No fear	Just born	Were up	See star
Go where	This year	Short goal	First one	Far away
Just married	My hero	Tore up	Bought skirt	Dog bark
Square dance	Hear you	Bore hole	Herd of sheep	Loud harp
Share toys	Near this	For him	Turn left	Love art
Dare you	Boat pier	No more	Learn skills	New car
Do care	Am hearing	White board	Never will	Start now
Not fair	Cheer on	Play sport	Spider web	Left arm
Cherry pie	Need gear	Corn on cob	Need butter	Guard house
No dairy	Buy souvenir	Big storm	Hurt knee	Garlic clove
Comb hair	Pay cashier	This morning	See dirt	Pink heart
Pet parrot	Eat cereal	Toy store	This girl	Visit farm
Finish marathon	Seems weird	Go north	New teacher	Dark chocolate
Carried away	Saw deer	Big fort	Eat dinner	Yard sale
Light fire	Need plier	Flat tire	Saw flier	Visit Ireland
Will hire	Phone wire	Admire you	In choir	Need to iron
Empire State Building	Feel tired	Baseball umpire	A liar	Phone wire

Table 4-23c. Vocalic /ɹ/	
Context: Sentence Level- Repeated Occurrence	
The <u>first</u> <u>girl</u> in line is the <u>winner</u>.	The <u>professor</u> said to <u>turn</u> it in <u>Saturday</u>.
<u>Stir</u> the <u>tart</u> <u>curds</u> in the soup.	<u>Pour</u> the <u>water</u> <u>over</u> the plants in the <u>garden</u>.
The <u>mirror</u> <u>near</u> the <u>door</u> is new.	My <u>favorite</u> <u>sport</u> is <u>soccer</u>.
They <u>cheered</u> <u>for</u> the <u>admired</u> <u>hero</u>.	Should I <u>wear</u> <u>shorts</u> <u>or</u> a <u>skirt</u> today?
<u>There</u> is a <u>storm</u> coming on the <u>north</u> <u>shore</u>.	Put <u>garlic</u> <u>butter</u> <u>over</u> the <u>asparagus</u>.
The cows <u>are</u> in the <u>farmyard</u> and the <u>barn</u>.	The <u>dark</u> <u>cherries</u> <u>are</u> <u>flavorful</u>.
The <u>orange</u> glaze and <u>turkey</u> go <u>together</u>.	<u>Her</u> <u>teacher</u> sent the <u>homework</u>.
<u>There</u> <u>are</u> <u>germs</u> in the <u>dirt</u> that can <u>hurt</u> you.	<u>Carl</u> is the <u>first-born</u> child.
My <u>first</u> <u>marathon</u> was in <u>Charlotte</u>, <u>NC</u>.	I think it's <u>fair</u> if you <u>care</u> to <u>share</u>.
<u>Where</u> <u>are</u> <u>your</u> pet <u>parrots</u>?	This is <u>their</u> <u>third</u> <u>year</u> of <u>marriage</u>.
The <u>guard</u> <u>works</u> at the <u>cherry</u> <u>farm</u>.	Be <u>sure</u> to <u>turn</u> <u>here</u> <u>before</u> you miss the house.
My <u>souvenir</u> in <u>Ireland</u> was <u>Merino</u> wool.	The seals <u>are</u> <u>near</u> <u>pier</u> <u>thirty</u>-nine.
The <u>toddler</u> asked <u>for</u> <u>more</u> <u>cereal</u>.	It was chilly <u>after</u> the <u>morning</u> <u>storm</u>.
We had <u>corn</u> and <u>celery</u> <u>for</u> <u>dinner</u>.	Ms. <u>Ferguson</u> is a <u>tired</u> <u>teacher</u>.
Use the <u>pliers</u> to cut the <u>hard</u> <u>wire</u>.	My <u>morning</u> <u>chores</u> <u>are</u> <u>very</u> <u>boring</u>.
I <u>hurt</u> my <u>arm</u> playing a <u>weird</u> <u>sport</u>.	It felt like a <u>very</u> <u>short</u> <u>year</u>.
The <u>army</u> <u>soldier</u> <u>carried</u> his heavy <u>gear</u>.	The <u>choir</u> <u>shared</u> the <u>flier</u> about the <u>concert</u>.
<u>There</u> <u>are</u> too many <u>irons</u> in the <u>fire</u>.	The <u>pyramids</u> in the <u>desert</u> <u>are</u> <u>covered</u> in <u>dirt</u>.
The <u>pitcher</u> called the <u>umpire</u> a <u>liar</u>.	I couldn't <u>start</u> my <u>car</u> in the <u>parking</u> lot.
The <u>store</u> <u>cashier</u> <u>worked</u> until midnight.	My left <u>tire</u> needs <u>more</u> <u>air</u>.

Table 4-23d. Vocalic /ɹ/
Context: Sentence Level- Single Occurrence

I left my <u>purse</u> on the stool.	<u>Dinner</u> will be exactly at 7:15.
Who won <u>first</u> and second place?	I want to see the <u>Pyramids</u> in Egypt.
The <u>Empire</u> State Building is tall.	The dog <u>walker</u> is going to be late.
I saw the info on a <u>flyer</u>.	My new <u>teacher</u> is Ms. Smith.
The <u>umpire</u> has a difficult job.	Joe will be <u>four</u> in July.
<u>Dessert</u> is the best thing of the day.	The <u>orange</u> glaze is delicious.
The mopped <u>floor</u> is still wet.	<u>Corn</u> is on sale at Safeway.
The <u>choir</u> show is this Monday.	The <u>spider</u> web is outside the window.
We went to <u>Ireland</u> last fall.	They think he is just a <u>liar</u>.
What <u>sports</u> do you like to play?	The big <u>storm</u> happened on Tuesday.
Can you <u>pour</u> me some juice?	She will be a big <u>star</u>!
I have a <u>fear</u> of heights.	The baby was <u>born</u> on Thanksgiving.
I have a <u>hair</u> appointment today.	My mom loves to cook with <u>garlic</u>.
Kevin has a pet <u>parrot</u> named Bill.	The <u>cherry</u> cake is the best.
I have a shelf of <u>souvenirs</u>.	Sometimes I eat <u>cereal</u> at night.
I was a <u>cashier</u> at Macy's.	I am planting daisies in the <u>yard</u>.
I need <u>butter</u> on my toast.	I <u>started</u> a new book last night.
Can you play the <u>harp</u> and piano?	They just got <u>married</u> in May.
This <u>year</u> will be a good one.	<u>Where</u> will you be this weekend?
The downtown <u>square</u> has shops.	I live <u>near</u> the bus stop.

Table 4-24. Common Patterns

This is a chart of commonly produced patterns by the most widely spoken languages in the world.
Consonant and vowel patterns are indicated below as <produced pattern/target sound in English>.
Conversations with native speakers, video recordings, and limited information from online sources were used to develop this.

*Deletion of Final Consonants (DFC)

Language	Consonants	Vowels	Grammar	Other
Amharic	Devoicing, DFC, r/ɹ (tapped), t/θ or s/θ, d/ð, z/ð	u/ʊ, o/a, ɛ/e	SVO word order, plurals, prefixes & suffixes	Omitting question words, epenthesis, syllable stress
Arabic	r/ɹ (trilled), b/p, v/f, t/t, d/d, r/ɹ (tapped, pre-vocalic), r/ɹ (trilled, post-vocalic), t/θ, d/ð	i/ɪ, u/ʊ, a/ə, e/ɛ	Articles, present verb tense + 'to be,' relative clauses	Epenthesis, focus words, monotone
Bengali	Initial blends, t/θ, d/ð devoicing, n/ŋ, r/ɹ (tapped), devoicing	u/ʊ, o/a	Pronouns, subject-verb agreement, suffixes & prefixes	Syllable stress, intonation, multiple meanings of words
Farsi	v/w, t/θ, d/ð, r/ɹ (tapped), devoicing	i/ɪ, u/ʊ, a/ə	Prepositions, prefixes & suffixes, plurals, adjectives, pronouns, articles	Epenthesis before initial /s/, syllable stress, intonation, volume
French	Omission of /h/, s/θ, z/ð, devoicing, ʃ/tʃ, ʒ/dʒ, r/ɹ (uvular), DFC	i/ɪ, a/æ, u/ʊ, o/a, ɛ/e, o/ɔ, a/ə	Verb tense, articles, adverbs, plurals	Syllable stress, intonation, rate of speech
German	Devoicing, v/w, t/θ, d/ð, r/ɹ (uvular), DFC	æ/ɛ, o/a, i/ɪ, u/o, o/a, ɛ/e	Gerund, verb tense, plurals, articles	Syllable stress, intonation, rate of speech
Hebrew	Devoicing, t/θ, d/ð, r/ɹ (uvular) or r/ɹ (trilled), omit /h/	i/ɪ, ɪ/i, ɛ/e, a/æ, a/ə, ʊ/u, ɪ/i	Verb tense, articles, gender nouns (i.e., aunt/uncle), plurals	Word linking, rate of speech, intonation, syllable stress, epenthesis
Hindi	w/v, v/w, t/θ, d/ð devoicing, n/ŋ, r/ɹ (tapped), t/t	ɛ/e, æ/ɛ, o/ɔ, i/ɪ, a/æ	Plurals, verb tense, articles, prepositions	Syllable stress, intonation, rate of speech, word linking

Language	Consonants	Vowels	Grammar	Other
Japanese	Deletion of /r/, l/r, r/l, b/v, h/f, devoicing, s/θ, d/ð, ʒ/dʒ	i/ɪ, ɪ/i, ɛ/e, ɛ/æ, o/ʌ, u/ʊ, a/o, o/a	Verb tense, idioms, prepositions, articles	Word linking, syllable stress, intonation, pausing, epenthesis
Korean	Devoicing, p/f, b/v, ɹ/l, l/ɹ, /w/ distortion, b/v, p/f, ʒ/dʒ, t/θ, d/ð	i/ɪ, ɪ/i, ɛ/e, ɛ/æ, o/ʌ, u/ʊ, a/o, o/a	Gerund, verb tense, plurals, articles, pronouns, adverbs	Syllable stress, intonation, thought groups
Mandarin	DFC, w/v, l/ɹ or w/ɹ, w/l or ɹ/l, t/θ or s/θ, d/ð or z/ð, n/ŋ devoicing, blends *l/n in Sichuan dialect	a/o, u/ʊ, i/ɪ, ɛ/e	Plurals, pronouns, gender confusion, articles, subject-verb agreement, prepositions	Syllable stress, intonation, word linking, epenthesis, rate of speech, omission of 'to be'
Portuguese	w/l (final), t/θ, d/ð, blends, devoicing, ʃ/tʃ, omit /h/	æ/ɛ, o/a, o/ɔ, i/ɪ, a/a, u/ʊ	Verbs ending in -ed, present-tense verbs, articles	Epenthesis before initial /s/, syllable stress, deletion of final /n/
Russian	w/v, v/w, t/θ, d/ð, devoicing (final), r/ɹ (tapped)	o/a, o/ɔ, i/ɪ, ɪ/i, u/ʊ, ɛ/æ	Articles, future tense verbs, prepositions	Syllable stress, intonation, wording linking
Spanish	b/v, r/ɹ (trilled), ʃ/tʃ, s/z, ʒ/dʒ, t/θ, d/ð, dʒ/j, DFC	i/ɪ, u/ʊ, a/ɑ, e/ɛ, a/æ, o/a	Verb tense, subject-verb agreement, subject omission	Focus words, syllable stress, monotone, epenthesis
Tagalog	b/v, p/f, s/z, t/θ, d/ð, tʃ/dʒ, ʃ/tʃ	i/ɪ, u/ʊ, a/a, o/a, a/æ	Verb tense, plurals, articles	Epenthesis, focus words, syllable stress
Turkish	Devoicing, w/v, v/w, t/θ, d/ð, r/ɹ (uvular)	a/o, o/a, u/ʊ, ʊ/u, i/ɪ, ɛ/e, i/e, o/ʌ	Prepositions, plurals, present-tense verbs, articles	Syllable stress, intonation, epenthesis
Vietnamese	Devoicing, t/θ, d/ð, deletion of /n/, l/n, deletion of /r/, ʒ/dʒ, blends, DFC	ɛ/æ, u/ʊ, o/ʌ, i/ɪ, ɪ/i, e/ɛ, o/a	Linking verbs, articles, pronouns, irregular verb tense	Word linking, syllable stress, intonation

Section 5

Suprasegmentals

Overview

Suprasegmentals refer to the elements of speech patterns that are above individual sounds. It gives languages their flow or rhythm. In accent modification, the following areas are often addressed:

- Rate of Speech, Pausing, Key Words
- Intonation
- Syllable Stress
- Word Linking
- Volume and Resonance

Intelligibility is most impacted by the articulation of consonants and vowels, while naturalness is most impacted by suprasegmentals. The rhythm of languages can be categorized into two categories: stress-timed languages and syllable-timed languages. Syllable-timed languages have syllables that are said at regular intervals, despite the context. Stress-timed languages have syllables that change based on stress and context. Table 5-1 is a chart to compare the features. Keep in mind that languages in each category exist along a continuum.

Feature	Stress-Timed Languages	Syllable-Timed Languages
Vowels	Stressed vowels are longer, louder, and higher. Unstressed vowels are reduced (shorter) and tend to converge as a schwa ('uh' sound).	Vowels have equal time, volume, and pitch. Vowels may seem more pronounced.
Syllable Structure	Syllables have a high amount of consonants and blends.	Syllables are open (end in a vowel) Fewer consonants in speech.
Key Words	Key words (usually the final word in a phrase) are emphasized: longer, louder, and higher. May sound more legato.	Key words are not emphasized; have equal stress as other words May sound more monotone & staccato.
Examples	**English**, Dutch, German	French, Mandarin, Spanish

Table 5-1. Stress-Timed vs. Syllable-Timed Languages

Rate of Speech

Different rates of speech are used in different settings. Generally, when engaging in a conversation, speakers should speak between 120-150 words per minute (WPM). Although, there is a range (120-260); the number varies by source. Typically, one will speak more quickly with friends or familiar conversational partners, than with unfamiliar conversational partners or in business settings.

A fast rate of speech impacts comprehension. A slow rate of speech impacts the interest of the listener. Both negatively impact the perceived naturalness of speech. It's typical for non-native speakers to feel that native English speakers speak at a very rapid rate. Sometimes, they may even try to increase their rate of speech to 'improve' naturalness. This doesn't help! The rate of speech varies by several factors.

The factors that impact the rate of speech are:
a. Complexity of the conversation
b. Level of familiarity with the listener
c. Nervous feelings
d. Conversational models growing up (e.g., parents speaking fast)

Discuss

Read the following prompts to the client and discuss their response.
1. When do you feel yourself using a fast rate of speech?
2. How do you feel when you use a fast rate of speech (e.g., tense, nervous, etc.)?

Pausing

One way to manage rate of speech and still sound natural when speaking is to pause in appropriate places in sentences. Pausing, also called thought groups, phrasing, or breath groups, is part of the rhythm of the English language. Most speakers are nervous about pausing. However, it's important for the:
- Meaning of messages
- Emphasis
- Listener comprehension
- Slowing rate of speech

Speakers should pause:
a. As a verbal comma
b. At the end of sentences

c. At the end of a thought group or phrase
d. To emphasize a key word

For speakers who find themselves using a lot of filler words (e.g., um, uh, like, so), just take a pause. The listener will appreciate the break, and this gives the speaker the chance to avoid a filler and think of their next word.

Discuss

Read the following sentences aloud to the client and pause for 1-2 seconds where there is a comma. Ask them to tell you where you paused and how it impacted the message.

1. I went to the store for milk, eggs, and bread
2. When did you, get back from your trip
3. Did you mean Disney World, or Disney Land
4. Where, were you
5. Here at this university, we have lots of students

Read these sentences aloud several more times and change up the pausing. Then discuss how pausing in different places impacts the message meaning, emphasis, listener comprehension, or effect. Have the client determine when pausing sounds more natural in sentences.

Key Words

As stated earlier, there are places to pause naturally in sentences for meaning or emphasis. The word before the pause is referred to as the key word. Key words are also called focus words or content words.
1. **Content Words:** nouns, verbs, adjectives, and adverbs.
2. **Function Words:** pronouns, articles, prepositions, quantifiers, and conjunctions.

Key words are usually the last content word in a phrase but can change for emphasis. They help you convey a message the way you want. The key word is usually followed by a pause to help with the meaning of the message and is stressed; the key word is longer, louder in volume, and higher in pitch. All the other words around the key word are shortened or combined.

Discuss

Read the sentences below aloud several times to the client and change up the key word. Discuss how the meaning changes.

1. She got a dog
2. Class is at 8:00 a.m.
3. We're meeting at 10:00 a.m.
4. The steaks are in the freezer
5. It was a great day

Then read the following sentences to your client and stress the **bolded** word. Ask them to tell you how the stressed word impacted the message (why was it stressed?).

Meaning	Examples
To answer a question	**Where** did you go? I went to the **store**. **Who** went to the store? **She** went to the store.
To correct information	Dan **went** to the movie. No, Dan **left** the movie.
Response with question	What did **you** think of the test? Fine, what did **you** think of the test?
To highlight contrast	She teaches at George **Washington** University but goes to school at George **Mason** University.
To exclude something	He **loves** dessert, but he **hates** chocolate.

Table 5-2. Key Words Examples

Word and Vowel Reductions

English is a stress-timed language, which means that key words are lengthened, while other words, usually the function words, in the phrase are shortened or combined. This is one reason non-native speakers assume that native speakers speak quickly.

I like to tell clients that native speakers 'smoosh' and 'slash' words. Meaning, they shorten and eliminate sounds and words as much as possible. For example, in the sentence, 'I went to the store,' if 'store' is the key word, it takes the speaker the same length of time to say, 'I went to the' as it does 'store.' Non-native speakers tend to pronounce each sound and word.

This also means that unstressed vowels are reduced, or shorter, and tend to become an 'uh' sound, which is called a schwa. In the same example as above, 'I went to the store,' the vowels in 'to' and 'the' are shortened to 'uh,' so the sentence sounds like 'I wentuh thuh store.'

If you have a difficult time hearing the key word, think about the one word in a phrase or sentence that cannot be 'smooshed' with the other ones. Below are words that are often reduced in connected speech.

Word	Becomes
to	'tuh'
was	'wuz'
the	'tha'
are	'er'
of	'uv'
a	'uh'
that	'thut'
for	'fer'
you	'ya'
at	'ut'
or	'er'
your, you're	'yer'

Table 5-3. Common Reductions

Discuss

Read the phrases aloud and have the client tell you where to reduce the vowel in the **bolded** word.

1. One **of** those
2. Need **a** break
3. She **was** late
4. **That's** terrible
5. What's **for** dinner
6. Knew **you** would
7. Meet **at** 6:00
8. **The** loud kids
9. Here's **your** money
10. Tea **or** coffee

<u>If the client is struggling with speaking too quickly, try this variation:</u>
1. Have the client focus on the movement of their articulators while speaking.

Rate of Speech Practice Stimuli

Remember the acronym **M.O.T.O.R.** Below is a suggestion for targeting key words.

	**Table 5-4. Formats for Practice**
	Word	**Instructor Utterance**	**Client Utterance**
M	**Model**	"I went tuh thuh **store**"- shortening non-stressed words, elongating key word	"I went tuh thuh **store**" - shortening non-stressed words, elongating key word
O	**Opposites**	"I went tuh thuh **store**"– target production "I went to the store" – no shortening of non-stressed words	"I went tuh thuh **store**"– target production "I went to the store" – no shortening of non-stressed words
T	**Tell apart**	"Are these the same or different: I went to the store I went to the store"	"Same"
O	**Over-Correction**	"I went tuh thuh **STORE**"- over-emphasizing key word and smooshing non-stressed words together	"I went tuh thuh **STORE**" - over-emphasizing key word and smooshing non-stressed words together
R	**Resay**	N/A	"I went tuh thuh **store**"

Section 1: Key Words and Pausing

Remember that the key word will change depending on the context.

Sentence Stimuli

Have the client read the sentences and stress the **bolded** key word and pause after (//) for emphasis. To make it feel more natural, add a statement or question to each sentence.

1. I want to meet with you on **Friday**// to go over the **homework**.
2. Is Disney World in **California**// or **Florida**?
3. My roommate **always** whistles// when he gets **home**.
4. I have two **dogs**// that live with my parents in **Alabama**.
5. She is looking forward to seeing her friends this **weekend**// and seeing **Hamilton**.

6. Please **silence** your phone// **before**// it wakes up the **baby**.

7. Did you know that there is a **pink beach**// in southern **Mexico**?

8. Will you be in **class** on Monday// to discuss **this**?

9. I have an **important** work call// **very** early tomorrow.

10. He's one of **those**//, the **lucky** ones.

11. She was **late** to the meeting//, **not** early.

12. Let's meet at **6:00**// **instead** of 8:00.

Have the client read these sentences aloud several more times and change up the key word. Respond with a follow-up statement based on the new meaning, so it flows like a short dialogue.

Q&A Stimuli
Have the client read the sentences and stress the **bolded** key word for emphasis.

1. Instructor: **Where** did you go?
   Client: I went to the **store**.

2. Instructor: **Who** went to the store?
   Client: **I** went to the store.

3. Instructor: Alex **went** to the office
   Client: No, Alex **left** the office.

4. Instructor: What did **you** think of the test?
   Client: **Fine**. What about **you**?

5. Instructor: Does she go to school at George **Washington**?
   Client: She teaches at George **Washington** but goes to school at George **Mason**.

6. Instructor: So, he **loves** desserts?
   Client: He **loves** desserts, but he **hates** candy.

7. Instructor: Are we meeting at **8:00**?
   Client: No, we are meeting at **6:00**.

8. Instructor: Did **you** like the play?
   Client: Yes, did **you** like the play?

9. Instructor: Are you going to Mexico in **April**?
   Client: No, we are going to Mexico in **June**.

10. Instructor: Was she **early** to the meeting?
    Client: She was **early** to the meeting but **late** to class.

Read the questions aloud several more times and change up the key word. Have the client respond with follow-up statements based on the new meaning, so it flows like a short dialogue.

Section 2: Reductions

Have the client read the phrases and sentences aloud while reducing unstressed vowels to a schwa and combining words. Words to combine are indicated with (-).

Phrase Stimuli

1. Should-have (should've)
2. Would-have (would've)
3. What-did-you (whadja)
4. A-lot-of (lotuv)
5. Sort-of (sortuv)
6. Have-to (have tuh)
7. Want-to (wanttuh)
8. For-you (fer ya)
9. It's-yours (it's yers)

Sentence Stimuli

1. You should-have tried the soup.

2. I would-have said no.

3. What-did-you do yesterday?

4. It-is sort-of formal.

5. I could-have done that faster.

6. We have-to make a quick call.

7. I want-to see the movie tonight.

8. It-is-a small gift for-you.

9. It-is yours if-you want it.

Section 3. Reading Passages

Have the client read the passages aloud while focusing on pausing after (//), emphasizing **bold** key words, and reducing unstressed words as indicated by (-). It is a lot to focus on at once, so clients may need to read the passage more than once and focus on each area individually.

Reading Passages- Short Stimuli

Reviews for Nutella:

1. If you-are reading-a review for-**Nutella**//, then you-have obviously never tried the-**stuff**//. If-you like hazelnut-and **chocolate**//, then you-will **love** this//.

2. I **love** this stuff//! We use it as-a dessert **treat**// due-to having-a food allergy in our **family**//. It-is great to be able to-purchase it **online**// and receive the-same product we would in the-**store**//. It arrived in one **package**// without any dents-or scratches.

Reviews for Banana Slicer:

3. I-have **always** wondered// how-to get that professional **restaurant** quality slice//. Now I **can**//! No more paying-for those expensively sliced **fruits**//. I can just stay- at **home**//.

4. What-an **amazing** product//. This year for-my **wedding** anniversary//, I asked what my wife **wanted**//. She told me after all-of these **years**//, I should know what she **wanted**//. Then-it **hit** me//, a-banana slicer//.

On My Way:

5. I-am on my way **home**//. First, I need-to stop at-the **grocery** store but should be home **by** 6:00//. Do we **need** anything//?

Reading Passages- Long Stimuli

Reviews for Nutella:

1. I haven't met-a person **yet**// that doesn't love **Nutella**//, and I don't think I **want-to**//. This stuff-is **simply** delicious//. I consider it-a pantry **staple**//, even though it's-a **guilty** pleasure//. It's great on **toast**//, with cream cheese on **bagels**//, on **ice cream**//, etc.// This jar-is extra-**large**//, larger than what I can find-in stores near **me**//. So, **hopefully**//, it should last-a **while**//.

2. If you-are reading-a review for-**Nutella**//, then you-have obviously never tried the **stuff**//. If-you like hazelnut-and **chocolate**//, then you-will **love** this//. I use it on toast, bagels, and **ice cream**//. **Sometimes**//, I put-a scoop or two in-a protein **shake**// or anywhere that-you might use **peanut butter**//. I ended up getting this small container for-a good **price**// on Amazon **Pantry**//.

Reviews for Banana Slicer:

3. What-an **amazing** product//. This year for-my **wedding** anniversary//, I asked what my wife **wanted**//. She told me after all-of these **years**//, I should know what she **wanted**//. Then-it **hit** me//, a-banana slicer//. Thank you so much for-making such a-fantastic and useful kitchen **tool**//. I am **sure**// that she-will always **treasure** it//.

4. I-was sitting on-the **couch**//, and my doorbell **rang**//. I leapt off-the sofa and ran-to-the door **screaming**//, "My banana **slicer**//!" I **opened**-the package// and **immediately** snatched-a banana to slice//. Without **instructions** included// I did-not realize I had to **peel** the banana first//. It was-a gooey **mess**//, and I had-to grab **another**//. This time I **peeled** it//.

On My Way:

5. I-am on my way **home**//. First, I need-to stop at-the **grocery** store but should be home **by** 6:00//. Do we **need** anything//? I think we-are out-of **milk** and **eggs**//. Do you want **skim**-or **whole** milk//?

Section 4. Spontaneous Speech

Short Spontaneous Speech Stimuli

See *Short Spontaneous Speech Starters* in section 6 for prompts.

Long Spontaneous Speech Stimuli

Engage the client in a short conversation (3-5 min) while focusing on rate of speech, pausing, key words, emphasis, and reductions. It's a lot to focus on at once, so be prepared to have several short conversations and focus on each area individually.

Intonation

If suprasegmentals give English its rhythm, intonation is the melody. Intonation is the rise and fall in pitch to convey a message. Intonation has 3 main functions to convey:

1. **Grammar**: asking a question vs. making a statement
2. **Meaning**: being genuine vs. sarcastic
3. **Emotions**: conveying one's mood (e.g., happy, sad, surprised)

The use of intonation to convey a message varies by language and culture. For example, in general, Spanish sounds more excited, and Japanese sounds more monotone. General American English (GenAm) is somewhere in the middle. Speakers of syllable-timed languages, or those that have a 'staccato' pattern, will tend to sound monotone. To compensate, these speakers may increase volume instead of changing pitch.

In GenAm, there are 4 types of intonation.

1. **Falling**: lowering the pitch at the end of a sentence
2. **Rising**: raising the pitch at the end of a sentence
3. **Falling-Rising:** lowering the pitch and then raising it at the end of a sentence
4. **Rising-Falling:** raising the pitch and then lowering it at the end of a sentence

There are general guidelines for when to use intonation, but there are no absolutes in intonation. Just like key words, it varies by context, speaker, and situation. There is a range of the rise and fall in pitch. The more emotion or emphasis behind the message, the higher or lower the pitch goes. Additionally, there are glides and step-ups/downs within words and pitch variations within sentences, especially longer ones with multiple thought groups. For words that are one syllable, there is a glide or pitch change within the single word at the end of a sentence or thought group. For words that are two or more syllables, there is a step up or step down from syllable to syllable within the word at the end of a sentence or thought group. Here are general guidelines for intonation.

1. Falling intonation is used to:
a. make a final comment (*He's very talented.*)
b. make a statement (*I live in Madrid.*)
c. ask a "wh" or how question (*What's next?*)
d. make a list (*We need milk, bread, and eggs.*)
e. confirm information; rhetorical questions (*How did I miss that.*)

f. add information to a statement (*My mom made bread today; she is famous for the recipe.*)

g. express understanding (*No, I don't have any questions.*)

2. Rising intonation is used to:

a. ask yes/no questions (*Is it hot outside?*)

b. convey unfinished thoughts or a statement (*I am available on Saturday, but....*)

c. ask for clarification/repetition (*Can you say that again?*)

d. ask tag questions to confirm information (*You're from Alabama, right?*)

e. to express uncertainty or doubt (*You said turn here?*)

3. Falling-rising intonation is used to:

a. show hesitation (*Well, sure, I guess that works.*)

b. make a statement (*I have homework to do.*) *as an alternative to falling intonation

c. give a choice (*Do you want tea or water?*)

d. make a list (*We need milk, bread, and eggs.*) *as an alternative to falling intonation

e. give polite introductions (*Hi, I'm Paul, and I will be your instructor.*)

4. Rising-falling intonation is used to show strong emotions such as:

a. surprise (*Oh wow!*)

b. anger (*I can't believe you did that!*)

c. enthusiasm (*We're going to the beach!*)

d. sarcasm (*It was a great day.*)

e. excitement or delight (*What an awesome trip!*)

Discuss

Repeat the next sentences four times, each with a different intonation to express a statement (falling), question (rising), show hesitation (falling-rising), or strong emotion (rising-falling). Discuss with your client how this changes the meaning of the sentence.

1. You went to the store on Saturday.

2. I need milk, pasta, and eggs.

3. Did you move?

Say the following sentences to the client aloud using intonation indicated in parentheses. The intended message is also indicated in paratheses. Have the client tell you if they hear rising, falling, falling-rising, or rising-falling intonation and discuss which sentences sound natural.

Typical intonation

a. She got a dog (statement, falling)

b. His name is John, right (tag question, rising)

c. Is it hot outside (yes/no question, rising)

d. He does know about it (statement, falling-rising)

e. I'm going to a meeting at 4:00 (final comment, falling)

f. I love the Mediterranean (excitement, rising-falling)

Atypical intonation

a. I want a dog (statement, rising)

b. What is your profession (wh question, rising-falling)

c. I did go to the show, but… (unfinished thought, falling)

d. Wow, where did you go (surprise, falling-rising)

e. You are Bob, right (tag question, falling)

If the client is struggling with intonation, try these variations:

2. Have the client hum the sentence after you say it to help them hear the melody.

3. Exaggerate your facial expressions to match the meaning you are trying to convey.

Intonation Practice Stimuli

Remember the acronym **M.O.T.O.R**. Below is a suggestion for targeting intonation using the formats.

	Format	Instructor Utterance	Client Utterance
		Table 5-5. Formats for Practice	
M	**Model**	"Are you hungry"- rising intonation	"Are you hungry"- rising intonation
O	**Opposites**	"Are you hungry"- rising intonation "Are you hungry"- falling intonation	"Are you hungry"- rising intonation "Are you hungry"- falling intonation
T	**Tell apart**	"Which one sounds like a yes/no question": "Are you hungry"- rising intonation "Are you hungry"- falling intonation	"First one, rising intonation"
O	**Over-Correction**	"Are you hungry"- over-emphasizing the rising intonation	"Are you hungry"- over-emphasizing the rising intonation
R	**Resay**	N/A	"Are you hungry"

Section 1: Emotions and Meaning

Sentence Stimuli

Read the list of emotions to the client.

Happy	Excited
Sad	Sarcastic
Shocked	Angry
Bored	Doubtful

Table 5-6. Emotions

Then have the client choose an emotion and read the sentences below using that emotion. Guess which emotions they chose. Do this several times and have the client choose a different emotion for each sentence. Then switch roles. The instructor reads the sentences aloud using different emotions and have the client guess the emotion.

1. It's time for class
2. She got a big dog
3. We had dinner at Ed's on Saturday
4. I'm going to Belize for the holiday
5. I have to get up at 4:00 a.m. tomorrow for a flight
6. I need to run to the store again
7. We're going to my aunt's house for the holidays
8. There are 3 puppies inside the fence
9. I saw him walk down the street
10. Sorry I was 15 minutes late

Section 2: Grammar

Have the client read the phrases and sentences aloud while practicing intonation patterns. Target intonation patterns are in parentheses.

End of a Statement Stimuli (falling intonation)

1. Yesterday was Tuesday
2. I had to run to the store
3. She prefers tea
4. I'm a student at the George Washington University
5. She was late to class
6. We have a meeting at 2:00
7. He was absent yesterday
8. The puppy needs a walk
9. Today is Monday
10. This week was ok

Lists Stimuli (falling-rising)

1. We're bringing dessert, spoons, and drinks
2. He speaks English, Spanish, and French
3. We need to pack our swimsuit, flip flops, and shorts
4. You can invite your friends, neighbors, and family
5. The icing has sugar, chocolate, and butter
6. The dog is part poodle, terrier, and lab
7. I am free on Monday, Tuesday, and Wednesday
8. I called my mom, sister, and brother
9. I have to clean, finish homework, and call home
10. I bought chips, salsa, and cheese

Question vs. List Stimuli (rising vs. falling-rising)

Read sentences below and have the client determine if it's a yes/no question (rising), either/or question (falling-rising), or an unfinished list (rising). Then switch roles. Have the client read, and the instructor determines the meaning.

1. Are you coming Friday or Saturday
2. Can we meet at 10 or 11
3. Are you from D.C. or Virginia
4. Do you like tea or coffee
5. Do you want dinner at 5 or 6
6. Did you go on a trip in April or May
7. Is his name Alex or Travis
8. Does he have a cat or dog
9. Is that a lab or retriever
10. Are you free today or tomorrow

Dialogue Stimuli

Decide who will be person A and person B. Read the dialogues several times using different intonations and discuss how the message changes.

1. New Puppy:
A: We have a new puppy
B: Oh, really?
A: Yes, it's a labradoodle
B: He is adorable

2. <u>Trip to Europe:</u>
A: I want to go to Europe soon
B: I hear it's lovely
A: You've been?
B: Yes, only to Germany

3. <u>Class:</u>
A: I really need to do my homework
B: Oh, we also have plans tonight
A: We do?
B: Yes, we can reschedule

4. <u>Dinner:</u>
A: What's for dinner?
B: Cereal
A: Cereal?
B: Yes, unless you feel like cooking

Section 3. Reading Passages

Have the client read passages aloud while focusing on intonation. Have the client change up the intonation and discuss how the meaning of the message changes.

Reading Passages- Short Stimuli

1. <u>Yesterday:</u>
Yesterday was quite busy. I had an unexpected call at 8:00 a.m. and then was 30 minutes late to work. On the way home, my car broke down, and I had to wait for 2 hours for roadside assistance.

2. <u>New Puppy:</u>
We have a new puppy. My husband surprised me for my birthday. Now we have to work on house training and separation anxiety.

3. <u>Holy Guacamole:</u>
Last night, we went to a Halloween party. There were lots of trick-or-treaters out dressed in costume. A small avocado jumped out of the bushes and screamed, "Holy guacamole." It was funny!

4. <u>We're Here:</u>

My sister came home from college yesterday. She brought her new friend home with her. As soon as they walked in after the long drive, she raised her hands and shouted, "We're here!"

5. <u>Old Business:</u>

The building on H Street is being torn down. There was a popular old business in there for 20 years. I guess we will see what opens in that space.

Reading Passages- Long stimuli

1. <u>Yesterday:</u>

Yesterday was quite busy. I had an unexpected call at 8:00 a.m. and then was 30 minutes late to work. On the way home, my car broke down, and I had to wait for 2 hours for roadside assistance. At least when I got home, my wife had dinner ready. Then I went to bed early.

2. <u>New Puppy:</u>

We have a new puppy. My husband surprised me for my birthday. Now we have to work on house training and separation anxiety. He doesn't sleep through the night. He has woken up at 3:00 a.m. every night this week. Oh boy!

3. <u>Holy Guacamole:</u>

Last night, we went to a Halloween party. There were lots of trick-or-treaters out dressed in costume. A small avocado jumped out of the bushes and screamed, "Holy guacamole." It was funny! We all had a good laugh. The party was a lot of fun, too.

4. <u>We're Here:</u>

My sister came home from college yesterday. She brought her new friend home with her. As soon as they walked in after the long drive, she raised her hands and shouted, "We're here." It was good to see her. The last time she was home this summer.

5. <u>Old Business:</u>

The building on H Street is being torn down. There was a popular old business in there for 20 years. I guess we will see what opens in that space. I'm hoping for a Chipotle. My friend wants a Starbucks.

Section 4. Spontaneous Speech

Short Spontaneous Speech Stimuli

See *Short Spontaneous Speech Starters* in section 6 for prompts.

Long Spontaneous Speech Stimuli

Engage client in a short conversation (3-5 min) while focusing on intonation to convey meaning, grammar, and emotions. It's a lot to focus on at once, so be prepared to have several short conversations and focus on each area individually.

Syllable Stress

In English, the average syllable length of words ranges from 1-6. In words with more than one syllable, stress is given to one syllable to form a rhythmic pattern and to indicate meaning. Stressed syllables are characterized by increased pitch, volume, and vowel length (like key words). Non-stressed syllables are shorter and often reduced to a schwa or 'uh' sound. Many people have difficulty identifying where the syllable stress is in words. One trick is to try to substitute a schwa for each syllable and see which one you cannot do so. That is the stressed syllable! Also, try this helpful website: https://www.HowManySyllables.Com/.

There are several rules and exceptions for syllable stress. Try to focus on how words sound, instead of memorizing the rules and exception.

1. For 2-syllable words
a. 1st syllable is stressed for nouns, adjectives, adverbs (*as in **doc**tor*)
b. 2nd syllable is stressed for verbs and prepositions (*as in ap**ply***)

Some words can be either a noun or a verb. The context and syllable stress are used to differentiate the meaning. Below are examples.

2-Syllable Nouns Stress the 1st syllable	2-Syllable Verbs Stress the 2nd syllable
a. **Ad**dict	a. A**ddict**
b. **Re**search	b. Re**search**
c. **De**fect	c. De**fect**
d. **In**crease	d. In**crease**
e. **Pro**gress	e. Pro**gress**
f. **Pro**duce	f. Pro**duce**

2. For 3+ Syllable Words
a. Words with prefixes- stress stays with the root word
   *as in sub**to**tal, co**pi**lot, disap**pear**, mis**guid**ed, overex**tend***

b. Words with the suffixes
   -ion, ial, ese, ity, ical, esque, ify, ic = stress is one syllable before the suffix
      *as in di**ges**tion, ex**haus**tion, spe**cif**ic*
   -gy, cy, ty, phy, fy, ate, ian = stress is two syllables before the suffix
      *as in **a**gency, a**pol**ogy, **dec**orate*
   -ee, ese, eer, esque = stress is on the suffix
      *as in employ**ee**, engin**eer**, Chin**ese***

Discuss

Read each word aloud and have the client count the number of syllables, which is indicated in parentheses.

No (1)

One (1)

Running (2)

Achievement (3)

Strength (1)

Photographic (4)

Photography (4)

Have the client listen to the following words and tell you if they have the same number of syllables or different numbers.

Word 1	Word 2	Answer Key
police	please	different
appear	appears	same
stretched	stretch	same
banana	bicycle	same
Hungary	hungry	different
nature	language	same
decided	decide	different

Table 5-7. Syllable Practice

Have the client listen to the following words and tell you which one has two syllables (**bolded** words).

1. cabinet ; day ; heart ; **address**
2. **fossil** ; purse ; left ; attention
3. popsicle ; **whistle** ; one ; sleeve

Have the client listen to the following words and tell you which one has 3 syllables (**bolded** words).

1. passing ; **medicine** ; juice ; racecar
2. **policeman** ; spinach ; stick ; fruitcake
3. secondary ; doughnut ; yellow ; **dinosaur**

Epenthesis

Refers to when a person adds an 'uh' sound in words. It adds a syllable to the word length, which can impact word meaning or syllable stress. Clients whose native language does not have many consonants or consonant blends may use epenthesis at the beginning or end of words (e.g., idea vs.ID) or in blends (e.g., suhlide vs. slide). Say the following pairs and ask the client how the words change when you add the syllable 'uh.'

Word	With Epenthesis
hungry	Hungary
please	police
ID	idea
notes	notice
decide	decided
Alex	Alexa

Table 5-8. Syllable Practice

Grammar

There are a few additional rules related to syllable stress and grammar, specifically for -ed and -s endings. Let's review them.

1. **For regular past tense –ed verbs**
   If the final sound is /t, d/ = add a syllable and pronounce –ed as /ɪd/
   as in painted, dated, waded
   All other voiced sounds = do not add a syllable and pronounce –ed as /d/
   as in pleased, moved, opened
   All other unvoiced sounds = do not add a syllable and pronounce –ed as /t/
   as in skipped, danced, picked

2. **For -s endings**
   If the final sound is /s, z, ʃ, ʒ, t͡ʃ, d͡ʒ/ = add a syllable and pronounce -s as /ɪz/
   as in wishes, guesses, catches
   All other voiced sounds = do not add syllable and pronounce –s as /z/
   as in rides, swims, begs
   All other unvoiced sounds = do not add syllable and pronounce –s as /s/
   as in speaks, hurts, drops

Syllable Deletion

For words with 3 or more syllables, English speakers may delete or 'drop' a syllable. Remember from the key words section, that native English speakers 'smoosh' and 'slash' words to shorten and eliminate sounds and words as much as possible. Syllable deletion has no rules and occurs irregularly. One must either listen carefully or try to memorize the words. It can also vary across U.S. dialects. Examples of words that have dropped syllables when spoken are:

Word	Becomes
Average	Av-rej
Beverage	Bev-rej
Chocolate	Chok-let
Difference	Dif-rence
Interesting	In-tresting
Restaurant	Rest-raunt

Table 5-9. Syllable Deletion

Compound Words

Compound nouns, verbs, and adjectives are formed when two or more words are combined to form a word with a new meaning. For example, white refers to a color, and house refers to a residence, but White House together refers to the residence of the U.S. President. Let's review the rules.

1. **Nouns**: Stress is on the first word in the compound
    as in *White House, nest egg*
2. **Verbs:** Stress is on the second word in the compound
    as in *outsmart, overdue*
3. **Adjectives:** Stress is on the second word in the compound
    as in *free-range, short-term*

If the client is struggling with syllables, try these variations:
1. Discuss root word and the rules that go with it
2. Have the client hum the word after you say it to hear the melody.
3. Have the client use a rubber band to stretch while elongating stressed syllables.
4. Have the client tap out each syllable and state which vowel cannot be replaced with schwa or 'uh' sound

5. Have the client place hand under their jaw and say a word to see which syllable forces their hand to move down the most

Syllable Stress Practice Stimuli

Below are stimuli for practicing syllable stress in short and long utterances. To build the client's motor planning, motor adaptation, and phonological awareness skills, remember the acronym **M.O.T.O.R**.

Below is a suggestion for targeting syllable stress using the formats.

Table 5-10. Formats for Practice			
	Format	**Instructor Utterance**	**Client Utterance**
M	**Model**	"**Doc**tor" - stressing first syllable	"**Doc**tor" - stressing first syllable
O	**Opposites**	"**Doc**tor" - stressing first syllable "Doc**tor**" - stressing second syllable	"**Doc**tor" - stressing first syllable "Doc**tor**" - stressing second syllable
T	**Tell apart**	"Are these the same or different:" "Doc**tor**" - stressing second syllable "**Doc**tor" - stressing first syllable	"Different"
O	**Over Correction**	"**DOC**tor" – emphasizing the loudness, length, and pitch of first syllable	"**DOC**tor" – emphasizing the loudness, length, and pitch of first syllable
R	**Resay**	N/A	"**Doc**tor"- stressing first syllable

Section 1: Syllable Stress

2-Syllable Words Stimuli

Have the client read the words aloud and discuss how the syllable stress changes for 2-syllable nouns vs. 2-syllable verbs. The stressed syllable is **bolded.** Remember that the stressed syllable is louder, longer, and higher.

Blocked

Nouns: *stress 1st syllable*	Verbs: *stress 2nd syllable*
1. **Ad**dict	1. **Ad**dict
2. **Re**search	2. Re**search**
3. **De**fect	3. De**fect**
4. **In**crease	4. In**crease**
5. **Pro**gress	5. Pro**gress**
6. **Pro**duce	6. Pro**duce**

Random

1. **Ac**tion	6. **Pa**per
2. **Buil**ding	7. **Con**cert
3. **Win**dow	8. A**chieve**
4. Ap**ply**	9. Suc**ceed**
5. De**stroy**	10. **Ap**ple

3+ Syllable Words Stimuli

Have the client read words aloud and make sure that the stressed syllable is louder, longer, and higher. The stressed syllable is **bolded.**

Blocked

Prefixes: *stays with root*	Suffixes: *Changes*
1. Sub**tot**al	1. Di**ges**tion
2. Co**pi**lot	2. Ex**haus**tion
3. Disap**pear**	4. **Ac**tivate
4. Mis**guid**ed	5. **Ed**ible
5. Overex**tend**	6. **Pol**icy

Random

1. Noncom**pli**ant	5. **Clar**ify
2. Redis**trib**ute	6. **All**ergy
3. Rear**range**	7. **At**rophy
4. Non**tox**ic	8. Cre**a**tion

Phrase Stimuli

Have the client read the phrases aloud and focus on the stressed syllable in the underlined word. The stressed syllable is **bolded.**

1. mis**guid**ed by the DMV
2. fresh **pro**duce
3. the non-com**pli**ant student
4. **com**pliment at work
5. are **ed**ible
6. more **re**search is needed
7. **buil**ding did not crack
8. rates will in**crease**
9. will ap**ply**
10. my **all**ergy

Sentence Stimuli

Have the client read the sentences aloud and focus on the stressed syllable in the underlined word. The stressed syllable is **bolded.**

1. I was mis**guid**ed by the DMV when I went to get my driver's license
2. I buy my fresh **pro**duce at Trader Joe's every week
3. The non-com**pli**ant student was expelled for plagiarism
4. He paid me a very nice **com**pliment at work
5. The beautiful flowers on the cake are **ed**ible
6. More **re**search is needed before my trip to Japan
7. The **buil**ding did not crack during the earthquake yesterday
8. The mortgage interest rates will in**crease** in 2 months
9. I must ap**ply** for the volunteer position and then interview
10. My **all**ergy to peanuts is very bad

Section 2: Grammar

Have the client read words aloud and convert them to past tense. Ask them which words have an extra syllable in the past tense.

-ed Endings Stimuli

Verb	Past Tense	Extra Syllable?
relax	relaxed	no
decide	decided	yes
need	needed	yes
attach	attached	no
organize	organized	no
change	changed	no
collide	collided	yes
calculate	calculated	yes
massage	massaged	no
reboot	rebooted	yes

-s Endings Stimuli

Verb	Past Tense	Extra Syllable?
splash	splashes	yes
allow	allows	no
sneeze	sneezes	yes
world	worlds	no
lemon	lemons	no
rash	rashes	yes
badge	badges	yes
skirt	skirts	no
garage	garages	yes
office	offices	yes

Section 3. Reading Passages

Reading Passages- Short & Long Stimuli

Short reading passage practice: Have the client read steps one at a time.

Long reading passage practice: Have the client read the full passage.

Multi-syllabic words are underlined, and the stressed syllable is **bolded.**

Betty **Cro**cker **Cho**colate Chip Cake **Re**cipe

1. Heat <u>**o**ven</u> to 350°F (325°F for dark or <u>**non**stick</u> pans). Spray <u>**bot**toms</u> and sides of 2 (8-inch) round cake pans with <u>**cook**ing</u> spray.

2. In a large bowl, beat cake mix, 1 ¼ cups milk, 1/3 cup <u>**melt**ed</u> <u>**but**ter</u>, and eggs with <u>e**lec**tric</u> <u>**mix**er</u> on <u>**me**dium</u> speed for 2 <u>**min**utes</u>, <u>**scrap**ing</u> the bowl <u>oc**ca**sionally</u>. Stir in ½ cup shaved <u>**choc**olate</u> <u>un**til**</u> just <u>**blen**ded</u>. <u>Di**vide**</u> <u>**e**venly</u> <u>be**tween**</u> pans.

3. Bake 28 to 32 <u>**min**utes</u> or <u>un**til**</u> a <u>**tooth**pick</u> <u>in**sert**ed</u> in the <u>**cen**ter</u> comes out clean. Cool 10 <u>**min**utes</u>; run <u>**met**al</u> <u>**spat**ula</u> <u>a**round**</u> the edge of pans to <u>**loos**en</u> cakes. <u>Re**move**</u> from pans and place on a <u>**cool**ing</u> rack. Cool <u>com**plete**ly</u> for <u>a**bout**</u> 1 hour.

4. In a large bowl, beat <u>**marsh**mallow</u> crème, 1 cup <u>**soft**ened</u> <u>**but**ter</u>, the <u>va**nil**la</u>, and 1 <u>**ta**blespoon</u> of milk with an <u>e**lec**tric</u> <u>**mix**er</u> on <u>**me**dium</u> speed <u>un**til**</u> <u>**blen**ded</u>. Beat in <u>**pow**dered</u> <u>**sug**ar</u> <u>un**til**</u> <u>**fluff**y</u>. If <u>**nec**essary</u>, beat in more milk <u>un**til**</u> the <u>**mix**ture</u> is thin <u>e**nough**</u> to spread. Stir in ¼ cup shaved <u>**choc**olate</u> <u>un**til**</u> <u>**blen**ded</u>.

5. Place one cake <u>**lay**er</u> on a <u>**serv**ing</u> plate. Spread ¾ cup <u>**frost**ing</u> on the top <u>**lay**er</u>, then top with the <u>**sec**ond</u> cake <u>**lay**er</u>. Frost the side and top of the cake with <u>re**main**ing</u> <u>**frost**ing</u>. With the <u>re**main**ing</u> 3 <u>**ta**blespoons</u> of shaved <u>**choc**olate</u>, <u>**sprin**kle</u> on top and sides of the cake.

6. Store <u>**loose**ly</u> <u>**cov**ered</u> in the <u>re**frig**erator</u>.
(Kitchens, 2018).

Section 4: Spontaneous Speech Stimuli

Short Spontaneous Speech Stimuli

See *Short Spontaneous Speech Starters* in section 6 for prompts.

Long Spontaneous Speech Stimuli

Engage the client in a short conversation (3-5 min) while focusing on the prosodic features (loudness, vowel length, pitch change) to emphasize syllable stress.

Word Linking

In connected speech, native English speakers link the end of one word to the beginning of the next word. This is what gives General American English the flow, or rhythm. Non-native speakers tend to pronounce each word separately.

If one is learning another language, word linking is what makes it difficult to understand native speakers because it's difficult to tell where one-word ends, and another begins. This is why native speakers sound like they are speaking very fast. To compensate, some non-native speakers may try to speed up their rate of speech, which will only increase a listener's confusion.

There are 3 rules for word linking.
1. **Final consonant to subsequent same consonant:** as in "Speaks Spanish"
   Produce the redundant consonant once (Speaks Spanish becomes SpeakSpanish)
2. **Final consonant to subsequent vowel:** as in "Wait up"
   Shift the final consonant to the next word (Wait up becomes Way-tup)
3. **Final vowel to subsequent vowel:** as in "May I"
   Insert 'y' or 'w' in between words (May I becomes May-yai)
   For words that end in 'u' or 'o' (front vowels), insert a "w"
   For words that end in 'e,' 'a,' or 'i' (back vowels), insert a "y"

Think about how a word is said, not spelled. For example, the word 'hour' is spelled with an 'h,' but when spoken, it starts with a vowel. When used in a phrase with a word that ends in a vowel, like 'two hours,' you would use the vowel to vowel linking rule and insert a 'w.' So 'two hours' becomes 'two-wours.'

Discuss

Have the client repeat the following sentences with and without word linking (indicated with /-/).
1. She speaks-Spanish well
2. Please wait-up for me
3. May-I have-a turn

Assimilation

Assimilation refers to sounds changing to be more similar to nearby sounds. For non-native speakers, this can also make it difficult to tell word boundaries (where one word ends, and another begins) and make the rate of speech seem faster. Below are basic 'rules' in General American English. Keep in mind that these rules can change based on context and emphasis.

'The'

There is a rule for the word 'the' and when to pronounce it as 'thee' and when to pronounce it as 'thuh.' It depends on the word that follows it. If the word 'the' is followed by a word that starts with a consonant, it is typically pronounced as 'thuh' as in 'thuh cat.' If the word 'the' is followed by a word that starts with a vowel, it is typically pronounced as 'thee' as in 'thee apple.' Of course, this varies by context and speaker, and either production is o.k. and will not impact the meaning of the message.

Discuss

Ask the client how they would pronounce 'the' before the following words (remember to link 'thee' with any vowel that follows with a 'y').
1. artist
2. professor
3. dog
4. hour
5. athlete
6. time
7. student
8. elephant
9. rules
10. class

Now have the client use these examples in sentences.

Glottal Stop for Final /t/

In most words that end in 't' that are followed by a word that starts with a consonant, the /t/ sound is dropped and replaced with what is called a 'glottal stop.' The easiest description of a glottal stop is that it's a sudden stop in airflow and voicing as in the phrase 'uh oh.' Just focus on dropping the 't' sound altogether at the end of words and replacing it with a sudden stop of air.

Discuss

First, have the client say, 'uh oh' and 'nuh uh' 3 times each.

Then ask the client how they would replace the 't' with a glottal stop in the following:

1. hot dog
2. meet me
3. get more
4. can sit
5. arrive late

Now have the client use these examples in sentences.

Reductions

As mentioned in the key words section, native English speakers reduce or combine the pronunciation of some words and phrases, making the utterance shorter and faster. Below are common examples.

Phrase	Becomes
Should have	Should've
Could have	Could've
Would have	Would've
Where did you get that	Where'd you get that
What will you have	What'll you have

Table 5-11. Common Reductions

Discuss

Ask the client how they would reduce the following:

1. sort of
2. a lot of
3. what did you do
4. who are you
5. what are these

Then have the client use these examples in sentences. After that, have the client say the sentences using reductions and then without (saying each full word). Discuss the differences.

Pronouns

Native English speakers reduce pronouns within phrases and sentences by omitting the first sound in the pronoun, which is typically 'h' or 'th.' So, for example:

Phrase	Becomes
Show him	Show im
Meet her	Meet er
Know them	Know em

Table 5-12. Pronoun Reduction Examples

Discuss

Ask the client how they would reduce the following:

1. did he
2. know her
3. give them
4. told her
5. see them

Then have the client use these examples in sentences. After that, have the client say the sentences using reductions and then without (saying each full word). Discuss the differences.

Elision

Elision refers to the deletion of a sound. In words that have triple clusters (3 consonants together as in 'desks'), one or more consonants are often deleted.

Word	Becomes
Sands	Sans
Months	Mons
Accepts	Acceps

Table 5-13. Elision Examples

Discuss

Ask the client how they would reduce the following:

1. tends
2. ducts

3. tents
4. hands
5. lends

Then have the client use these examples in sentences. After that, have the client say the sentences using reductions and then without (saying each consonant in the cluster). Discuss the differences.

If the client has difficulty with word linking, try this variation.
1. Have the client draw a diagram on the stimuli page to note when to link words.

Word Linking Practice Stimuli

Remember the acronym **M.O.T.O.R**. Below is a suggestion for targeting word linking using the formats.

	Table 5-14. Formats for Practice		
	Format	**Instructor Utterance**	**Client Utterance**
M	**Model**	"Please way-tup for me"- linking wait-up	"Please way-tup for me"- linking wait-up
O	**Opposites**	"Please way-tup for me"- linking wait-up "Please wait up for me" – saying each word separately	"Please way-tup for me"- linking wait-up "Please wait up for me" – saying each word separately
T	**Tell apart**	"Which one has the linked phrase:" "Please way-tup for me"- linking wait-up "Please wait up for me" – saying each word separately	"First one"
O	**Over-Correction**	"Please waaaay-tup for me"- over-emphasizing moving the final consonant from 'wait' to 'up'	"Please waaaay-tup for me"- over-emphasizing moving the final consonant from 'wait' to 'up'
R	**Resay**	N/A	"Please way-tup for me"

Section 1: Word Linking

Phrase Stimuli

Have the client read the phrases using co-articulation to link words together.

Consonant-Consonant	Consonant-Vowel	Vowel-Vowel
Speaks Spanish	Pick up	Go on
Wait to	Bring in	We are
What time	Brown eyes	Blue eyes
This says	Stand on	We ate
Let's see	Is expected	I eat
Turned down	Good evening	Know it
Big game	Good idea	Who is
Can never	Like it	So excited
Good day	Get up	Buy one
This Saturday	Kicked out	May I

Sentence Stimuli

Have the client read the sentences using co-articulation to link words together. Your answer key is below; /-/ indicates linking words.

1. She speaks-Spanish very well.

2. We will wait-to-order for 5 minutes.

3. Please pick-up the trash that fell from your bag.

4. Go-on-and tell me what happened.

5. I know-it will be-a fun-event.

6. I'm so-excited to see Hamilton-on Broadway.

7. That's-a good-idea that Steven had.

8. My football team has-a big-game this-Saturday.

9. We-ate-at Founding Farmers last night for dinner.

10. I had to stand-on the stool to reach the cup.

Section 2: Assimilation

Time Stimuli

Have the client read the times aloud and use co-articulation to link words together where applicable.

1. 9:38 (nine thirty-eight)
2. 10:05 (ten-oh five)
3. 11:30 (eleven thirty)
4. 12:03 (twelve-oh three)
5. 2:08 (two-oh-eight)
6. 7:40 (seven forty)
7. 4:07 (four-oh seven)
8. 3:03 (three-oh three)
9. 1:09 (one-oh nine)
10. 5:02 (five-oh two)

Final /t/ Stimuli

Have the client replace /t/ as a glottal stop in each phrase.

1. eat soon
2. wait here
3. put down
4. it says
5. at home
6. that dog
7. what now
8. don't care
9. dirt floor
10. not now

You & I Stimuli

Have the client say 'you' and then 'I' in front of each word and focus on using 'y' or 'w' to link the two words.

1. eat
2. open
3. owe
4. adapt
5. adore
6. invest
7. act
8. awoke
9. eat
10. explain

The + Word Stimuli

Have the client put 'the' before each word and focus on using "thee" or "thuh" to link the two words.

1. way
2. ability
3. internet
4. hour
5. movie
6. people
7. problem
8. idea
9. oven
10. exam

Pronouns Stimuli

Have the client reduce the pronouns in the following phrases by omitting 'h' or 'th.'

1. call him
2. with them
3. did he
4. not her
5. with him
6. know him
7. see her
8. need them
9. not his
10. got them

Elision Stimuli

Have the client reduce the triple consonant clusters in the following phrases.

1. air ducts
2. two months
3. accepts cash
4. white sands
5. lends money
6. tends garden
7. wants more
8. hunts rabbits
9. spends energy
10. new hints

Section 3. Reading Passages

Have the client read the following passages and focus on co-articulation to link words together as well as assimilation.

Reading Passages- Short Stimuli

1. Class:
Today, we have class-at 8-05. The professor-emailed to say she-is running late. So-I get-to sleep-in-an-extra 5 minutes!

2. Thanksgiving:
For Thanksgiving, we will be visiting family. I love the holidays! We will-eat-turkey, potatoes, cranberry relish,-and chocolate cake.

3. Work:
My boss called to say there has been-an-error. We went through each line-of the data. However, we couldn't find the source.

4. Happy:
The fall makes me happy. I love the crisp leaves,-apple cider,-and pumpkin flavors. The temperature-is perfect-too.

5. Email:

I emailed her to-ask-about her availability. The email bounced back though. I will wait-to contact her-again.

Reading Passages- Long Stimuli

1. Harry Potter Synopsis:

In the adaptation-of the first-of J.K. Rowling's popular children's novels-about Harry Potter, a boy learns-on his-eleventh birthday that he-is the orphaned son-of two powerful wizards-and possesses-unique magical powers-of his own. He-is-summoned from his life-as-an-unwanted child to become-a student-at Hogwarts, an-English boarding school for wizards. There, he meets-several friends who become his closest-allies-and help him discover the truth-about his parents' mysterious deaths.

2. Great British Bake-Off Wikipedia Synopsis:

The Great British Bake-Off is-a British television baking competition, produced by Love Productions, in which-a group-of-amateur bakers compete-against-each-other-in-a series-of rounds, attempting to impress-a group-of judges with their baking skills with-a contestant being-eliminated-in-each round and the winner being selected from the contestants who reach the finals. The show's first-episode was-aired-on-August 17, 2010, with-its first four series broadcast-on BBC Two, until-its growing popularity led the BBC to move-it-to BBC-One for the next three series.

3. Workshop:

Thanks for volunteering for the workshop this week! Below is the-agenda-and-attached-are more resources for you. This workshop-is hosted by the-English for-Academic Purposes (EAP) department,-and you can view-all-of the workshops-offered-at the library-on their website. I-encourage you to review them beforehand. Please let me know-if you have-any questions. Email-is the best way to reach me.

4. Birthday Dinner:

Autumn-is celebrating her birthday-on Thursday-and we want-to make-it extra special. We'd love for you to join her for dinner-at New Bar-at the Wharf-in DC. Reservation-is-at 7:30 pm. If you happen to get there before-us, the reservation-is-under my name. But there-are two tables.

5. Email:

It was nice-seeing you-all today! See below for-a recap-of the next steps. Starting September 16,-our weekly track meetings will be Thursdays from ten to-eleven-a.m.-eastern time. Check the syllabus for-exact dates because we won't meet-every Thursday. Track meetings will be-in person-in Phillips Hall. If you-are unable to make-it due to-illness, please-send me-an-email.

Section 4. Spontaneous Speech

Short Spontaneous Speech Stimuli

See *Short Spontaneous Speech Starters* in section 6 for prompts.

Long Spontaneous Speech Stimuli

Engage the client in a short conversation (3-5 min) while focusing on co-articulation to link words together and assimilation. It's a lot to focus on at once, so be prepared to have several short conversations and focus on each area individually.

Resonance and Volume

The resonance and volume of a person's voice impact intelligibility and can vary across language and culture. Since resonance can impact volume, or specifically the ability to increase volume, these two topics are addressed together.

Volume

Volume refers to the loudness or softness of your voice. It is the most obvious vocal element noticed of a speaker. Volume can also vary based on personality, culture, and languages spoken. For effective communication, a speaker should speak at a level so the listener can hear them, and that is comfortable for the listener's ears.

It's helpful to think of a rating scale of 1-5, with 1 being very quiet (a whisper) and 5 being very loud (shouting). Naturally quiet speakers should try to speak at a level 4, and their volume will be perceived as a level 3. Naturally loudspeakers should try to speak at a level 2, and their volume will be perceived as a level 3.

Of course, the level of volume that is appropriate can vary across scenarios: the size of audience, size of the room, background noise, etc. For large audiences and rooms, speakers should use a microphone, so they do not have to strain their voice.

Discuss

Ask the client in what scenarios they would need to speak at a level 1, 2, 3, 4, and 5. (e.g., library, 1:1 conversation, social settings, presentation, sporting event)

Then engage in short conversations with the client. Have the client practice using lower and higher volume levels throughout the conversation and rate their level of volume. Then switch roles. Discuss how the volume impacts the speaker and listener.

If the client has difficulty with volume, try these variations:
1. Have the client sit with both feet on the floor and push down into the floor to increase their volume
2. Have the client stand up and move closer or farther away from you and have them adjust their volume accordingly
3. Refer to the 1-5 rating scale throughout sessions and have the client practice speaking using all volume levels

Resonance

Resonance refers to the airflow as it passes through the pharyngeal (throat), oral (mouth), and nasal (nose) cavities. General American English resonates in the middle of the oral cavity. Other accents may use a more pharyngeal resonance or nasal resonance. For example, French and Spanish are considered languages with a nasal resonance, and sound nasal. Tagalog and Arabic are considered languages with a pharyngeal resonance, and sound throaty or chesty. Resonance can also be impacted by the size and shape of the oral cavity and vocal tract of individuals.

A quick test for nasal resonance is to have the client plug their nose and count from 1-20. If there is no difference in oral and nasal sounds, the client is most likely using a nasal resonance.

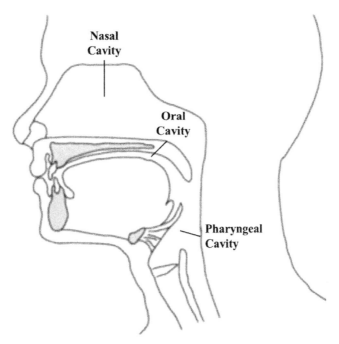

Figure 5-1. Resonance Diagram

Professional speech resonates from the pharyngeal and oral cavities. Think of these two types of resonance as working together to help you maintain optimal pitch and a more powerful voice. Volume and resonance are closely related because it's easier to project your voice using an oral and pharyngeal resonance, than nasal.

Discuss

Have the client sit up tall and take 5 deep belly breaths. If needed, have them use a prop, such as a clipboard, against their stomach. While taking deep breaths, the belly and prop should visibly move back and forth.

After the belly breaths, tell the client to focus on loose and buzzy lips while saying the following stimuli and focus on where they feel the vibration. The client needs to take one breath per utterance. While producing oral resonance, the client will feel a vibration in the oral cavity, not the nose. Have client practice by saying the following.

1. A sustained 'mmm'
2. A sustained 'mmm' + vowel (e.g., ma, my, me, moo)
3. Numbers 1-10
4. Days of the week
5. Months of the year
6. /m/ words (e.g., maybe, money, more, my, mine)
7. /m/ words in phrases (e.g., make more money)

If the client is struggling with resonance, try these variations.

1. Use sustained /n/
2. Use other sustained consonants
3. Use sustained vowel
4. Change pitch during sustained sound productions
5. Have client plug nose and say above stimuli #1-6. Listen for differences in the production of oral and nasal sounds. The client should focus on feeling different sensations for oral and nasal sounds (e.g., blocked air pressure on nasal sounds, buzzy lips on oral sounds).
6. Straw Phonation: Have the client stick straw into a glass without water. While blowing into the straw, have the client produce sound, starting monotone and then changing pitch. Repeat and have the client move from sounds to words and phrases (Above stimuli #2-6). Add water to the glass for more challenge.
7. Resonance Hand: Have the client place 4 fingers from one hand over their mouth vertically and produce a sustained 'mmm,' then have the client slowly pull their hand away from their mouth. Have the client repeat this with words and phrases (Above stimuli #2-6) and fewer fingers each trial.
8. If the instructor or client suspects that they have a true voice disorder, the client must be referred to a Speech-Language Pathologist (SLP) or Otolaryngologist (ENT) for assessment and treatment.

Vocal Hygiene

Vocal hygiene is a term that refers to healthy vocal habits. Here are strategies:

1. Stay hydrated by drinking plenty of water.
2. Take vocal rests from talking throughout the day.
3. Maintain an appropriate volume level throughout the day (e.g., avoid whispering, shouting, and excessive throat clearing).
4. Sit across from communication partners
5. Use an upright, relaxed posture when sitting and standing throughout the day to decrease tension on your neck and increase breath support

Volume and Resonance Practice Stimuli

Remember the acronym **M.O.T.O.R**. Below is a suggestion for targeting resonance using the formats.

<table>
<tr><th colspan="4">Table 5-15. Formats for Practice</th></tr>
<tr><th></th><th>Format</th><th>Instructor Utterance</th><th>Client Utterance</th></tr>
<tr><td>M</td><td>Model</td><td>"Make more money"- with oral resonance</td><td>"Make more money"- with oral resonance</td></tr>
<tr><td>O</td><td>Opposites</td><td>"Make more money"- with oral resonance

"Make more money"- with nasal resonance</td><td>"Make more money"- with oral resonance

"Make more money"- with nasal resonance</td></tr>
<tr><td>T</td><td>Tell apart</td><td>"Are these the same or different: Make more money"- with oral resonance

"Make more money"- with nasal resonance</td><td>"Different"</td></tr>
<tr><td>O</td><td>Over-Correction</td><td>"Make more money"- holding out the /m/ with buzzy lips</td><td>"Make more money"- holding out the /m/ with buzzy lips</td></tr>
<tr><td>R</td><td>Resay</td><td>N/A</td><td>"Make more money"</td></tr>
</table>

Section 1: Volume and Resonance

Have the client read the phrases with a sustained /m/ and level 3 volume.

Phrase Stimuli

1. My way
2. Maybe today
3. Maybe later
4. Most likely
5. More on that
6. Make more money
7. Monday is best
8. Macaroni and cheese
9. Medium or large
10. Mint chocolate chip

Q&A Stimuli

1a. Instructor: Which way?
1b. Client: My way

2a. Instructor: When will you do that?
2b. Client: Maybe today

3a. Instructor: Can we try now?
3b. Client: Maybe later

4a. Instructor: Are you attending the party?
4b. Client: Most likely

5a. Instructor: Does that make sense?
5b. Client: More on that

6a. Instructor: What is the goal?
6b. Client: Make more money

7a. Instructor: Which day do you prefer?
7b. Client: Monday is best

8a. Instructor: What will you have?
8b. Client: Macaroni and cheese

9a. Instructor: What sizes do they have?
9b. Client: Medium or large

10a. Instructor: What kind of ice cream is that?
10b. Client: Mint chocolate chip

Sentence Stimuli
1. I'm on my way to New York City.
2. Maybe today we can see a show.
3. Maybe later we can grab dinner.
4. Most likely, I will return tomorrow.
5. I'll send more on that later.
6. I want to make more money this year.
7. Monday is best for the meeting.
8. We had macaroni and cheese for dinner.
9. Do you want a medium or large?
10. I don't like mint chocolate chip!

Section 2. Reading Passages

Have the client read the following passages and focus on a level 3volume and oral resonance.

Reading Passages- Short Stimuli

1. <u>On My Way:</u>
I'm on my way to New York City. Maybe today we can see a show. Maybe later we can grab dinner. Most likely, I will return tomorrow.

2. <u>More on That Later:</u>
I'll send more on that later. Maybe Monday I will have time. What time will you be in the office? I believe I have your email.

3. <u>Macaroni and Cheese:</u>
We ate at Martha and Murphy's for dinner. They have the best macaroni and cheese. It has mushrooms and maple syrup.

4. <u>Medium or Large:</u>
Every time you go to a coffee shop, they ask you what size. I can never decide between a medium or large. I asked myself, 'Do I want to save calories or money?'.

5. <u>Make More Money</u>:

Doesn't everyone want to make more money? My dream job would be to get paid to watch puppies, read magazines, and travel the world. What about you?

Reading Passage- Long Stimuli

1. <u>On My Way</u>:

I'm on my way to New York City. Maybe today we can see a show. Maybe later we can grab dinner. Most likely, I will see Mamma Mia on Monday. I will return tomorrow with macadamia nut muffins for mom.

2. <u>More on That Later</u>:

I'll send more on that later. Maybe Monday I will have time. What time will you be in the office? I believe I have your email. Check your email first thing in the morning. If you do not see it, make sure you tell me.

3. <u>Macaroni and Cheese</u>:

We ate at Martha and Murphy's for dinner. They have the best macaroni and cheese. It has mushrooms and maple syrup. My friend prefers the mandarin macaroons. I highly recommend this place. It is on Madison Avenue, next to Mia's.

4. <u>Medium or Large</u>:

Every time you go to a coffee shop, they ask you what size. I can never decide between a medium or large. I asked myself, 'Do I want to save calories or money?'. I like to try the new menu item each Monday. At the moment, they have a matcha mocha.

5. <u>Make More Money</u>:

Doesn't everyone want to make more money? My dream job would be to get paid to watch puppies, read magazines, and travel the world. I would love to visit Morocco, Mexico, and Mali in the next year. I would invite all my friends to visit. Maybe they can stay for the summer. What about you?

Section 4. Spontaneous Speech

Short Spontaneous Speech Stimuli

See *Short Spontaneous Speech Starters* in section 6 for prompts.

Long Spontaneous Speech Stimuli

Engage the client in a short conversation (3-5 min) while focusing on a level 3 volume and oral resonance.

Table 5-19 is a chart of commonly spoken languages organized by resonance patterns. Conversations with native speakers, video recordings, and limited information from other sources were used to develop this chart.

Table 5-16. Resonance Patterns of Most Commonly Spoken Languages			
Language	**Nasal**	**Oral**	**Pharyngeal**
Arabic			X
Bengali			X
Chinese Mandarin	X		
English		X	
Ethiopian		X	
French	X		
German			X
Hebrew			X
Hindi			X
Japanese	X		
Korean	X		
Persian			X
Portuguese	X		
Russian			X
Spanish	X		
Tagalog			X
Turkish			X
Vietnamese	X		

Section 6

Session Materials

Suggested Activities

Below are suggested activities organized by each context level. Most of these can be used for any topic area covered. As the client becomes familiar with each target, change the setting. Conversations don't happen in a vacuum, and clients need to practice in a variety of situations with a variety of partners.

Isolation and Syllables

1. Drill
2. Opposites (negative practice, minimal pairs)
3. Tell apart (auditory discrimination)
4. Over-correction
5. Use as warm-up

Words

6. Drill
7. Opposites (negative practice, minimal pairs)
8. Tell apart (auditory discrimination)
9. Over-correction
10. Generate a list of commonly used words
11. Brainstorm topics or words that will be used in a given social situation
12. Use as warm-up
13. Play games such as memory or bingo
14. Say a set of numbers (odds, evens, set of 10 that includes target)
15. Say days of week and months of the year

Phrases

16. Drill
17. Opposites (negative practice, minimal pairs)
18. Tell apart (auditory discrimination)
19. Over-correction
20. Generate a list of commonly used statements
21. Read idioms
22. Brainstorm phrases that will be used in a given social situation
23. Choose 3 phrases to use tomorrow
24. Practice social phrases to wish someone a good weekend

Sentences

25. Drill
26. Opposites (negative practice, minimal pairs)
27. Tell apart (auditory discrimination)
28. Over-correction
29. Generate a list of commonly used statements
30. Brainstorm sentences that will be used in a given social situation
31. Practice asking for a check at a restaurant
32. Role-play ending a phone conversation
33. Role-play asking a friend to a social event such as lunch or dinner

Reading Passages (short)

34. Read tweets
35. Read a menu
36. Read 2-3 sentences at a time from an article
37. Read song lyrics (parts)
38. Read short emails
39. Read lines from a play
40. Read customer reviews online (Amazon, Etsy, etc.)
41. Read book/movie reviews
42. Read synopsis of books/movies
43. Read news headlines
44. Read memes
45. Read comic strips
46. Read directions on packaging
47. Read Facebook posts
48. Read tongue twisters

49. Read jokes or riddles
50. Read closed captioning on a video

Reading Passages (long)

51. Read news article
52. Read long emails
53. Read from a blog
54. Read from a textbook
55. Read from a book
56. Read recipes
57. Read song lyrics (full)
58. Read a magazine article
59. Read comic books
60. Read a brochure or pamphlet
61. Read children's book

Spontaneous Speech (short)

62. Order from a menu (use different cuisines)
63. Describe symptoms to a doctor
64. Role-play a mock interview
65. Practice asking a friend to make plans
66. Summarize a favorite book
67. Summarize a day/week
68. Summarize a current event
69. Discuss an article or book read (Q&A)
70. Discuss a favorite movie
71. Practice small talk
72. Record voicemail greeting weekly
73. Choose 3 things to say….tomorrow, this week, at work, in class, etc.
74. Role-play picking up a prescription
75. Practice ordering coffee in person
76. Role-play asking for help/service in a store
77. Walk to a nearby business and ask a question
78. Practice parts of a long conversation
79. Practice introducing self at an event
80. Describe the meaning of idioms and use them in an example
81. Play a card or board game suitable for adults that involve Q&A
82. Give directions to a place
83. Make or change airline reservations

84. Order office supplies
85. Discuss charts (e.g., charts of dog breeds, periodic table, plants, etc.)
86. Read aloud flyers with upcoming activities

Spontaneous Speech (long)

87. Describe directions to home from here
88. Describe how to make a favorite meal
89. Discuss a current event
90. Practice giving a presentation
91. Practice giving a speech
92. Role-play leading a lab meeting
93. Role-play leading a small group meeting
94. Describe a favorite trip
95. Describe an ideal weekend
96. Describe a favorite game
97. Describe a favorite sport
98. Role-play a phone call
99. Role-play talking to customer service about an issue
100. Have the client teach you about their area of expertise
101. Bring in a conversation partner
102. Confirm phone number or email address
103. Role-play office hour appointment
104. Practice leaving a telephone message
105. Story retell
106. Picture description
107. Pretend to be a tour guide
108. Pretend to be a volunteer guide at a local festival or attraction
109. Describe a trip
110. Describe your ideal job
111. Describe an ideal day
112. Describe an average day
113. Pretend to be on a board and role-play a planning meeting

Short Spontaneous Speech Sample Prompts

Below are prompts for eliciting short spontaneous speech samples (1-3 sentences) from your client. There are 15-20 prompts in each of the following categories:

Describe how-to: Ask the client to describe how they would complete a given task.

Describe your: Ask the client to describe a given prompt.

Describe what you would do if: Ask the client to describe what they would do in a given scenario.

State your opinion: Ask the client to state their opinion on a given topic.

Wh questions: Ask the client to answer who, where, when, what, and why questions.

Would you rather: Ask the client what they would prefer between two given choices and state why they would choose it.

Interview practice questions: Ask the client to answer practice interview questions.

Describe How-To
In 1-3 sentences, describe how to….
Make your favorite snack
Sew a button
Deposit a check
Get to your house
Order from a restaurant
Train for a marathon
Train for a triathlon
Play your favorite game
Do your favorite dance
Paint a wall
Send a text message
Order an Uber
Wash your hands
Parallel Park
Make a sandwich
Brush your teeth
Plant a garden
Change a lightbulb
Choose an outfit
Tie your shoes

Describe Your
In 1-3 sentences, describe your….
Favorite meal
Favorite city
Favorite memory
Favorite trip
Favorite outfit
Favorite celebrity
Favorite book
Favorite movie
Favorite show
House
Car
Best friend
Family
Neighborhood
Pet
Fashion sense
Hobby
Schedule
Classes/Job
Weirdest dream

Describe What You Would Do If
In 1-3 sentences, tell me what you would do if....
Your car broke down
Your friend canceled plans at the last minute
You spilled water on your computer
Your jacket zipper broke
You broke your sunglasses
You forgot your umbrella
You overslept
You forgot your wallet
You cracked your phone
Witnessed a theft
You forgot you had an exam
You forgot to wish your friend a happy birthday
You forgot to get milk at the store
Your friends threw you a surprise party
You missed the last evening train
You forgot your computer charger
You found a $100 bill
The waitress undercharged you
You forgot your email password
You lost a $20 bill

State Your Opinion
In 1-3 sentences, state your opinion on….
Social media
Taking a gap year
Living abroad
Black tie events
Halloween
Traveling solo
American sports
American food/diet
American fashion
Scary movies
Eating dessert for breakfast
Cruises
Bitcoins
Ghosts
Buying a house vs. renting
Smoking in public places
Household chores
Teaching handwriting in schools
Public transportation
Free education

Wh Questions
In 1-3 sentences, answer these questions….
Who cleans your teeth (e.g., "A dentist cleans your teeth")
Who cares for sick animals
Who works in outer space
Who fixes cars
Who writes novels
Where do you find a swimming pool
Where do you buy groceries
Where do you check out books
Where do you mail packages
Where do you exercise
What has a bulb
What has an engine and wings
What has a door and windows
What has soil and plants
What is soft and fluffy
When do you eat breakfast
When do you eat lunch
When do you eat dinner
When do you sleep
When do you exercise
Why do we eat
Why do we sleep
Why do we exercise
Why do we work
Why do we watch TV

Would You Rather
In 1-3 sentences, answer these questions....
Would you rather fly or drive and why
Would you rather meet an alien or robot and why
Would you rather go into the past or the future and why
Would you rather be able to speak all foreign languages or be invisible and why
Would you rather go without internet or your phone and why
Would you rather be Batman or Spiderman and why
Would you rather call a friend or text them and why
Would you rather go bungee jumping or skydiving and why
Would you rather work in a group or alone and why
Would you rather be on an island alone or with someone who talks nonstop and why
Would you rather be too hot or too cold and why
Would you rather go to Alaska or Hawaii and why
Would you rather have an older or younger sibling and why
Would you rather be really busy or really bored and why
Would you rather watch a big game on TV or in person and why
Would you rather be super late or super early and why
Would you rather have your own boat or your own plane and why
Would you rather eat pizza or salad for the rest of your life and why
Would you rather have a hit song or novel and why
Would you rather be older or younger and why

Interview Practice Questions
In 1-3 sentences, answer these interview questions….
What are your strengths
What are your weaknesses
Why did you choose this profession
Where do you see yourself in 5 years
Who is your mentor and why
Tell me about a conflict you faced and you how dealt with it
Tell me about a mistake you made and how you dealt with it
What are you looking for in a job
How do you prioritize your schedule/obligations
Are you willing to relocate
What questions do you have about the job
What is your dream job
Tell me about an accomplishment you are proud of
Describe yourself
What motivates you
What are you looking for in a leader
Describe your learning style
Describe a time when you had to adapt your plans at the last minute
Do you prefer to work in a team or alone and why
What do you know about your (desired) profession

Section 7

Professional Speaking

Professional speaking refers to speaking a way that others think of as competent, reliable, and respectful. What is considered professional or respectful can vary across cultures, country regions, and generations. This topic area is helpful to address with clients from other countries as well as clients from the U.S. Professional speaking is also a great opportunity to pull together segmental and suprasegmental targets and address them in longer utterances and conversation as well as discuss cultural norms. Topics addressed in professional speaking may include:

- Body Language
- Grammar
- Small talk
- Phone Effectiveness
- Humor

Some or all these topics may feel overwhelming for a non-native speaker as they navigate work, academic, and social situations. However, they are important to learn as professional communication skills are highly sought after by employers. These skills can be acquired through practice.

Body Language

Communication is more than words. In conversation, listener's focus on nonverbal communication, or body language, to interpret what a speaker is saying. For example, a listener may say that they are interested in the topic, but their body language may show disengagement (e.g., the body is turned away from the speaker, looking around the room).

Understanding nonverbal communication is essential in interpreting a speaker's intended message. This is why messages in texts or email can easily be misinterpreted. Nonverbal communication can vary across cultures, leading to communication breakdowns between conversation partners. There are a few key areas to think about.

Personal Space

Personal space refers to the area around a person they view as their own. It's also the space where one feels comfortable when talking to or being next to another person. The distance between oneself and others varies greatly between cultures. In the U.S., general rules are:

- **Close distance:** 1 foot for close, intimate relationships
- **Friendly distance:** 1-4 feet (arms-length) for people you know such as friends, co-workers, and family
- **Social distance:** 3-10 feet for casual acquaintances and co-workers
- **Public distance:** 12 feet or more in public spaces

When talking with someone, if the other person backs away a little, they likely feel you are getting too close to their comfort zone. Be mindful of the other person's preferences and not try to close the gap. Some cultures prefer more or less personal space compared to others, so don't be surprised if a communicative partner moves closer or farther away during the conversation.

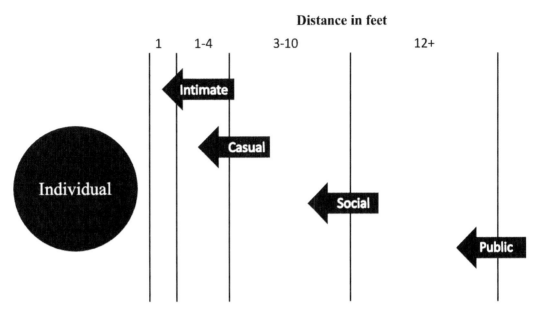

Figure 7.1 Personal Spaces for Social Interaction

Discuss

Ask the client how they would describe their comfort level with personal space in the following scenarios and discuss their responses.

- With an instructor
- With friends
- With professors or colleagues
- With their boss
- With strangers

Eye Contact

Eye contact can vary across cultures, so it's important to consider your audience and their expectations when speaking. It is important to give eye contact because it builds rapport and connection with the communicative partner or audience. Too much eye contact can be viewed as threatening, and too little eye contact can be viewed as uninterested or disrespectful. It can feel awkward to look someone in the eye. One trick is to visualize a T on the other person's face, with the top line connecting the eyebrows and the lower line extending to the lips. Shift the gaze along the T.

Generally, in the U.S., people are most comfortable with eye contact being held for 2-5 seconds, which is roughly 1-2 sentences in length. However, eye contact varies by the size of the group in which you are speaking.

a. **<u>One-on-One and Small Group Conversations:</u>** More eye contact is o.k. for conversations with one person or small groups. With the conversational partner/s, maintain eye contact for 4-5 seconds, look away briefly, and then return the gaze. In a small group, be sure to use eye contact with each person in the group. This will help them feel connected.

b. **<u>Large Group or Presentation:</u>** For presentations to a large audience, it's impossible to make eye contact with everyone in the room. Speakers should scan the room to move their focus across the audience throughout the presentation. Some speakers will move their eyes in a figure-8 pattern by looking at all four corners and the center of the audience. If the presentation is recorded, chances are this is where the cameras will be. So, two birds, one stone!

When possible, move around the room to help listeners feel connected. If someone asks a question, maintain eye contact with that person when answering and face your body (head, shoulders, feet) towards them. Also, moving towards the listeners will help them feel more captivated.

It can be very intimidating to speak in front of a large audience. To increase one's comfort level with eye contact (and in general), scan the room before a presentation as a quick 'eye warm-up.' For the warm-up, take a few seconds before a presentation to move your eyes around the room and hold your gaze on a spot for 2-5 seconds.

Discuss

Ask the client to think of a rating scale of 1-5, with 1 being very uncomfortable and 5 being very comfortable, and where their comfort level would fall on this scale in the following scenarios. Then discuss their responses.

- With an instructor
- With friends
- With professors or colleagues
- With their boss
- With strangers

Posture

Like eye contact and volume, posture can convey a message to the listener. Slouching can convey a lack of interest or decreased confidence. Stand or siting up tall during conversations or presentations is important to show interest and respect. More space between your shoulders and head will make a person look less tense. Sitting or standing tall will also help maintain an appropriate volume when speaking.

Face the listener, and as a good rule of thumb, the toes, torso, and shoulders should be facing them to visually show that you are attentive to them. Keep arms loose and moving away from the body to show comfort and trust.

Gestures

It's common for people to gesture or talk with their hands while speaking. Gestures can help both the listener and speaker follow the conversation. For the speaker, gestures can help them think of words, speak concisely, add emphasis, and be perceived as energetic and warm. For the listener, gestures can help them understand the message and retain two times as much information.

There are a few rules to consider about using gestures.
- **Use gestures mindfully:** Too many gestures can be very distracting and look more like an interpretive dance. Too few gestures can make the conversation or presentation seem boring
- **Gestures should match the message:** Gestures used should relate to the topic and add to the message, not distract from it. For example, if talking about an increase in something, have hands go up or wide to show 'increase'
- **Keep fingers together:** In a more formal setting, keeping fingers 'webbed' together will make the gestures appear more controlled
- **Keep palms up and open:** Always keep hands palm up, never palm down, to appear open and approachable

Another important gesture involves the mouth, not the hands, and that is smiling! An authentic smile can convey enthusiasm, confidence, and interest. Try it out.

Additionally, read the listener's gestures to interpret their level of interest. In social settings, when approaching a group of people, look for people with their feet turned outward. They are going to be more open to someone else joining their conversation. In conversation with others, look for an eyebrow raise and maintained eye contact to indicate a strong interest in the topic.

Body Language Practice Stimuli

Have the client maintain a short conversation or practice giving a short presentation while focusing on body language as well as segmentals and suprasegmentals previously targeted. It's a good idea to practice these skills in conversation in different ways. Have the client practice skills as discussed and then again, the "opposite way" or against what is expected. Then discuss how this impacted the listener and the speaker.

Grammar

Grammar is an area that varies based on the client's individual needs. Some clients may have difficulty with grammar in writing as well as speaking. For accent modification and professional speaking, it's important to focus on the grammatical difficulties in speech. Each client will have various strengths and weaknesses regarding grammar. Based on informal observations in conversation, determine if there are any patterns with grammatical difficulties. Earlier in the book, the most common patterns organized by language are organized in Table 4-24.

Below is a list of common grammatical difficulties of English language learners.

- Misuse or omitting of articles (a, an, the)
- Using incorrect verb tense
- Using incorrect prepositions
- Confusing gerunds (adding -ing) and infinitives ('to' form of a verb)
- Confusing adverbs and adjectives (e.g., speak good vs. speak well)
- Using incorrect subject-verb agreement
- Using incorrect word order (e.g., car blue vs. blue car)
- Using plurals incorrectly

Grammar Practice Stimuli

Ask the client what areas of grammar they feel they struggle with and would like more help. The client may need to address one or more of these. Have the client maintain a short conversation or practice giving a short presentation. It's a good idea to practice these skills in conversation in different ways. Have the client practice skills as discussed and then again, the "opposite way" or against what is expected. Then discuss how this impacted the listener and the speaker. See *Suggested Activities* in section 6 for more suggestions.

Small Talk

Small talk refers to a polite conversation in a 1:1 or social setting. The topics are usually unimportant and uncontroversial. The purpose of small talk is to build a relationship between acquaintances or colleagues. Here are a few rules to keep small talk going:

- **Ask open-ended questions:** Avoid yes/no questions and ask wh questions to get more information from the speaker. For example, instead of 'Do you like Harry Potter?' one can ask, 'What do you think of Harry Potter?'
- **Give more information:** Sharing information shows an interest in talking with the conversation partner. It also gives the conversation partner a chance to find something in common or something they can ask more about
- **Start with a general topic:** A general topic is something that most people can relate to or understand (e.g., ask about work, day, sports, weather, current events)
- **Ask follow-up questions:** To show interest and keep the conversation going, ask the conversational partner questions about themselves or the topic

Discuss

Read the following prompts to the client and discuss their responses.

1. What types of situations do you frequently find yourself in that require the use of small talk?
2. List examples of topics that are appropriate (e.g., weather, current events, weekend plans) vs. topics that are not appropriate (e.g., religion, politics).

Small Talk Practice Stimuli

Role-play small talk with your client. It may help to imagine being in a scenario in which small talk is expected (e.g., job interview, happy hour, meeting a new acquaintance). Try to keep the conversation going for 3-5 minutes.

It's a good idea to practice these skills in conversation in different ways. Have the client practice skills as discussed and then again, the "opposite way" or against what is expected. Then discuss how this impacted the listener and the speaker.

Phone Effectiveness

It may be more difficult for a listener to understand someone when speaking on the phone. A big reason is that there are no visual cues to help with comprehension. Listeners rely a lot more on visual cues than they realize.

There are a few things to keep in mind to increase effective communication over the phone, especially if there are concerns about speaking intelligibility.

- Speak slightly slower than the usual rate
- Introduce yourself and state the purpose of the call
- For informal conversations, incorporate small talk into beginning and end of the call
- State the upcoming topic and use descriptive language to give context clues
- Restate important information to confirm details, such as times and dates
- If intelligibility is a real concern, try to over-articulate sounds in words.

Phone Effectiveness Practice Stimuli

Have clients rehearse their portion of a phone call to a friend, relative, or business and focus on all segmental and suprasegmental areas previously addressed. Another idea for practice is to have the client rehearse their voicemail greeting and change it up frequently.

It's a good idea to practice these skills in conversation in different ways. Have the client practice skills as discussed and then again, the "opposite way" or against what is expected. Then discuss how this impacted the listener and the speaker.

Humor

Humor has its time and place in almost all interactions. Using humor appropriately can help build relationships, reduce stress, and help get the point across. Of course, the use and delivery of humor can vary greatly across cultures, settings, and generations. As you continue with connected speech, try to use slang, sarcasm, and idioms throughout sessions with clients. Encourage the client to use these as well.

Sarcasm

Sarcasm is a type of humor that usually makes fun of someone or something. It's a verbal statement that means the opposite of what is happening, but facial expression and intonation convey the sarcastic intent. Sarcasm is often used with native English speakers in the U.S. It's also heard frequently in TV shows and movies. Here are examples of when you may use or hear sarcasm.

1. **When someone says something obvious:** For example, two people are walking to work in the rain. One says, "it's very wet outside." The other says sarcastically, "Tell me something I don't know!"
2. **When somebody does something wrong:** For example, a driver makes a wrong turn and gets lost. The passenger says, "Great job."
3. **When something bad happens to you:** For example, you break your favorite glass and say, "Well, that's just perfect."
4. **When something unsurprising happens:** For example, a friend leaves her bike parked out front of a store unlocked, and when she returns, it is missing. You ask, "You didn't see that coming?"

Because sarcasm can hurt people's feelings, one must be careful when and how often it is used. Sarcasm should not be used in professional settings or interpersonal relationships as this could have the opposite effect and have negative consequences. It can be viewed as disrespectful or unsympathetic.

Discuss

Read the following prompts to the client and discuss their responses.

1. Have the client come up with examples of when they heard sarcasm (e.g., in conversations, TV, movies). Ask them to explain the scenario and if the sarcasm was funny or hurt someone's feelings.
2. Have the client list settings/scenarios in which it is ok to use sarcasm and when it is not (think of at least 5 each).

Slang

Slang refers to vocabulary (words or phrases) that is considered informal and typically limited to a region or group of people. It can even be limited to a specific situation or profession. The use of slang reflects a culture and helps convey thought and meaning while connecting with peers. Since it is limited to a region, it's similar to dialects, in that meaning and use can vary across the U.S. Because slang is considered to be informal, it's best used in social settings, not formal or business settings (unless it's related to the profession).

Slang Practice Stimuli

Review common slang words or phrases and their meaning. Then, engage the client in a dialogue using slang terms. Examples are below, but terms are constantly changing. There are many more online.

1. **A-game:** best self
2. **Blow/bomb:** to fail or perform poorly
3. **Bro**: a male friend (often used by other males)
4. **Cash/buck:** money
5. **Chill:** relax
6. **FYI:** acronym for 'for your information'
7. **Spill the tea:** gossip
8. **LOL:** laugh out loud
9. **Easy peasy/easy breezy:** easy or effortless
10. **Ride shotgun:** ride in the front passenger seat in a car
11. **Rip off:** to be overcharged
12. **Screw up:** to make a mistake
13. **Chit chat:** have a casual conversation (small talk)
14. **Hit the spot:** food or drink that was really good, just what you wanted
15. **What's up:** another way to ask 'how are you'
16. **24/7:** non-stop, around the clock
17. **Wicked:** amazing
18. **Wrap-up:** to finish or bring to an end
19. **When pigs fly:** It will never happen
20. **Lit:** Amazing or cool

Idioms

An idiom is a phrase whose meaning is different from the literal interpretation. It's similar to slang in that expressions can be regional and help convey meaning or thoughts. Although, popular idioms do not change as much as slang. Unlike slang and sarcasm, it's ok to use idioms in professional or business settings to help get the point across.

Idioms Practice Stimuli

Review idioms and meanings. Then, engage the client in a dialogue using the idioms. Examples are below, there are lots more examples online.

1. **Add insult to injury:** Make a bad situation even worse
2. **Piece of cake:** easy or effortless
3. **See eye to eye:** Two (or more people) agree on something
4. **Missed the boat:** Someone missed their chance at something
5. **Kill 2 birds with 1 stone:** To do two things at the same time
6. **On the ball:** A very responsible, efficient person
7. **Cut corners:** When something is done badly to save money
8. **Costs an arm and a leg:** When something is very expensive
9. **The last straw:** A further annoyance or problem in a series of unfortunate events that make it unbearable
10. **On the fence:** When someone does not want to choose or make a decision
11. **Feeling under the weather:** Feeling sick, unwell
12. **Speak of the devil:** When the person you have just been talking about arrives
13. **Break a leg:** Wishing someone luck
14. **Hit the nail on the head:** A correct, precise answer
15. **Can't judge a book by its cover:** Something is different than how it appears, usually for the better
16. **Bite off more than you can chew:** Take on too much work or responsibility
17. **Get the hang of it:** Getting used to something, understanding the process
18. **Once in a blue moon:** infrequently/rarely
19. **Butterflies in my stomach:** Feeling extremely nervous
20. **At the drop of a hat:** To do something immediately

Section 8

Summary

There is so much to learn and explore with accent modification. This book is a compilation of everything I wish I knew when I began working with clients, from assessments to coaching sessions.

The resources in this book are meant to get you started in determining goals and working with your clients. Of course, no two clients are alike. Some will respond best to learning features of GenAm individually and others may prefer focusing on several all at once, like the overall rhythmic pattern. Some clients may prefer technical jargon and diagrams (e.g., the vowel chart), while others may do best with instructor modeling and imitation.

I have included additional resources for your convenience, such as websites, books, and podcasts. I encourage you to use all these resources to be creative in coming up with your own techniques and materials too.

Accent modification is a journey taken together by both the instructor and client. For instructors, working with clients to achieve their goals enriches their understanding of diversity in the world of speech and elevates their ability to continue helping others professionally. For clients, the same journey sends them on a path of self-awareness and discovery towards more effective communication with others, an increase in their self-esteem, and potential new personal and professional possibilities.

I hope that you always keep exploring and growing. I wish you all the best in your journey in accent modification!

Please reach out with any questions or comments: Kari@GlobalSpeechTherapy.Com.

There is a companion website that contains downloadable Word documents of the assessment materials and practice stimuli for you and your own clients.

You can access the companion website at
https://GlobalSpeechTherapy.Com/AccentBook
Password: Accent12345

Additional Resources

Websites:

American Speech-Language-Hearing Association (ASHA)
  https://www.asha.org/public/speech/development/Accent-Modification/
Corporate Speech Solutions https://www.corporatespeechsolutions.com/
Corspan http://www.corspan.org/
David Alan Stern https://learnaccent.com/
Dialect and Accent Archive https://www.dialectsarchive.com/dialects-accents
Dynamic Dialects Accent Chart https://www.dynamicdialects.ac.uk/accent-chart/
English Accent Coach https://englishaccentcoach.com/
English Current https://www.englishcurrent.com/
Global Speech Therapy Blog https://globalspeechtherapy.com/blog/
Home Speech Home https://www.home-speech-home.com/speech-therapy-word-
  lists.html
Interactive Learning Modules
  https://www.rit.edu/ntid/slpros/assessment/speechvoice/eval/7
IPA Keyboard https://ipa.typeit.org/full/
Language and Country Project http://www.ritell.org/Language-and-Country-Projects
Language Manuals http://languagemanuals.weebly.com/language-manuals-list.html
Learn to Present https://learntopresent.com/
Phonemic Inventories Across Languages
  https://www.asha.org/practice/multicultural/Phono/
Science of People https://www.scienceofpeople.com/
Speech Accent Archive https://accent.gmu.edu/
Tools for Clear Services https://tfcs.baruch.cuny.edu/consonants-vowels/
Voice and Speech Trainers Association (VASTA) https://vasta.org/

YouTube Channels:

Rachel's English https://www.youtube.com/c/rachelsenglish
Elemental English https://www.youtube.com/c/eLeMentalEnglish
Jennifer ESL https://www.youtube.com/c/Englishwithjennifer
Sounds American https://www.youtube.com/c/SoundsAmerican

Podcasts:

Visceral Voice https://www.thevisceralvoice.com/podcast
In a Manner of Speaking https://www.paulmeier.com/in-a-manner-of-speaking/
Lingthusiasm https://lingthusiasm.com/

Social Media:

SLPs in Accent Modification Facebook page
  https://www.facebook.com/groups/543299812453471/

Online Courses:

Teaching American English Pronunciation https://www.udemy.com/course/teaching-american-english-pronunciation/?referralCode=110AC39E7B6016E6F935

Core Principles of Accent Modification
https://www.udemy.com/course/core-principles-of-accent-modification/?referralCode=FB60F759DC13BED873D6

Books:

Here's How to Do Accent Modification: A Manual for Speech-Language Pathologists
  Author: Robert McKinney
Mastering the American Accent
  Author: Lisa Mojsin

Printed in Great Britain
by Amazon

82872269R00147